UNCOUPLING

AN INSIDER'S GUIDE TO SEPARATION IN NEW ZEALAND

BARBARA RELPH

Copyright © 2021 Barbara Relph

Barbara Relph asserts her moral right to be identified as the author of this work.

All rights reserved. No part of this publication may be produced or transmitted in any form or by any means, electronic or mechanical, including photocopying, recording or information storage and retrieval systems, without permission in writing from the copyright holder.

Published by BarbWire

Website: www.uncoupling.guide

A catalogue record for this book is available from the National Library of New Zealand.

ISBN 978-0-473-58303-3 (paperback)

ISBN 978-0-473-58304-0 (EPUB)

Cover design by Georgia Shattky

CONTENTS

Introduction	vii
Author's Note	ix
Are you sure this what you want?	1

PART 1
THE IMMEDIATE ISSUES

Conversations you never wanted to have and how to have them	7
Children come first	11
Where will you live?	21
Are pets children?	25

PART 2
AIMING FOR EMOTIONAL REGULATION

Are you coping?	31
Grieving what you have lost	33
Getting help — coaching and counselling	37

PART 3
COMMUNICATING

Communicating better with your former partner	45
People other than your former partner and your children	51
Closing the door on abusive or controlling behaviour	57

PART 4
WHAT NOW? REACHING AGREEMENT

Resolving your dispute	63
New Zealand law	79

Lawyers and legal advice	97
The cost of separation	103

PART 5
CREATING YOUR NEW (BEST) LIFE

Taking care of yourself	109
What do you want from your new life?	115
Taking control of your financial life	119
Taking control of your work life	129
Taking control of your love life	139
A new relationship (without the old problems)	157
Checklist for separation	165
The last word	169
Acknowledgments	171
About the Author	173

PRAISE FOR UNCOUPLING

I worked with Barbara for several years to achieve financial separation and was very pleased to be asked to review the legal section of Uncoupling. *I took the opportunity to read the entire book, and I believe it to be an enormously useful resource for women and men at any stage of the separation process.*

When we met for the first time, post-financial settlement, I was delighted to see Barbara looking so well and happy, making the most of her writing and research skills, and putting her personal experiences to excellent use. I commented that it seemed separation was the best thing that ever happened to her. She agreed.

I see clients every day who would benefit from Uncoupling. *I couldn't have written it better myself.*

ANTONIA FISHER QC, RELATIONSHIP PROPERTY SPECIALIST

INTRODUCTION

My relationship was 33 years old at the time it ended in 2017. In the years that followed there was angst and heartache as my former partner and I uncoupled not only our finances and assets, but what our ongoing future personal relationship would look like, and our separate relationships with our adult children.

Having emerged on the other side, through trial and error rather than wisdom, I can now look back on how I thought it would work out with a wry smile. I was completely wrong. I had no idea what I would go through to untangle myself from my previous life.

I am quietly proud of my new life — a new career, a different and more evolved relationship with my children, and a new partner. I have established new friendships and rekindled old ones, and I know where I stand financially. I also have a lot of new attitudes.

Because it's only possible to experience one side of the equation, my personal standpoint necessarily leads to some natural bias, which I have made every effort to curb. I was the one to leave my relationship. I also had privileges many will not have — I had financial support from my former partner to help me get through the first 18 months post separation. I didn't have dependent children, and I don't have housing or ongoing serious financial issues. Recognising many do not have these advantages, I sought other viewpoints, and these have been incorporated.

I write this not as an expert — far from it — but as a woman who got a lot of things wrong. Many experts were consulted, separation stories swapped, and much research carried out, especially in the law and those facets of separation I didn't personally experience.

Along the way I frequently searched for guidance, but there were few practical resources. So, I thought I would write one. For you.

AUTHOR'S NOTE

In this book you will find information on many aspects of separation in New Zealand, from how to talk to your partner and children about separation to resolution options and the legal nitty-gritty, and finally to coming out the other side in good shape to start your new life.

Personal stories in each section provide candid, real-life illustrations of the various issues addressed. Because the stories are so personal, real names are not used.

Not everything in this book will apply to every uncoupling, so use the table of contents to pick and choose, depending on what stage you are at in the process.

Whether you are considering separation, are years into the process, or are emerging out the other side, you will find useful, practical, and encouraging information here. You are among friends.

ARE YOU SURE THIS WHAT YOU WANT?

SOMEONE HAS TO ASK. If you are the person considering making the announcement to your partner (and the world), have you thought through the ramifications of what's about to happen? If you haven't quite got there yet, counselling can help you work through the issues without pre-destination. At the very least a counsellor can advise on just how to approach the conversation with your partner, family, and friends with a view to minimising the harm to them.

The effect on your life will be momentous. Your financial security will likely be upended; your partner possibly devastated; and there will be a lot of stress and change in your future. The effect on others around you should not be underestimated. The degree of impact on children and the wider family may take you by surprise.

However, we don't get second chances in life and your happiness must also be taken into account. If you have no appetite for continuing the relationship, reading this is as good a place to start as any.

PART 1
THE IMMEDIATE ISSUES

Whether you are the person who ended the relationship or the one who was left makes a huge difference to how you manage your separation.

No matter the circumstances, there's generally one person who makes the decision to leave. That person may have been on an emotional rollercoaster for some time already and has had the opportunity to process the ending of the relationship, even before setting separation in motion. They may have plans and possibly even feel hopeful or excited about what life will hold for them after leaving the relationship. They may also, however, be fearful and grieving, despite knowing it is for the best.

The person who is left can be completely shocked and even humiliated, maybe feeling they have failed. Not only have their future plans been turned completely upside down in an instant, but they are faced with working through their grief and recreating their life in a more public forum than their partner. The resentment and blame which may follow casts the person who is left as the victim in the eyes of others. Put simply, for there to be a victim, the person who left must be a villain, right? Actually, no.

The role of victim doesn't always come naturally, and many will feel uncomfortable being assigned that role. They may not want the separation to define them socially, especially when they didn't invite the event or want the attention.

Relationships are, of course, significantly more complex than victims and villains and the spectrum of attitudes and emotions is vast. In all relationships, there are two sides to the story, and many reasons relationships fail. Rarely is one party solely responsible for the breakdown of the relationship. One thing is certain: there are no winners at the time of separation.

You will find yourself faced with many decisions. You will need to talk to someone — who can you trust to share this with? Do you need a lawyer? And if so, when do you need a lawyer? Critically for many, where is the money going to come from, or am I responsible for continuing to pay my partner's living expenses? Where will you live? What about pets? And clearly, if you have children, their needs are of primary concern in all of these questions.

Slow down and make a list of issues you need to deal with. You will most likely need to discuss many of these issues with your former partner, ideally in person, ideally calmly.

There's no doubt about it, making these decisions is not only extremely difficult while in this emotional state, but it is also frightening.

CONVERSATIONS YOU NEVER WANTED TO HAVE AND HOW TO HAVE THEM

RESOLVING to separate was the hardest and biggest decision of my life and I know I am not alone in this. Depending on the situation, separation can have ramifications well beyond the direct relationship. Financial advisers will strongly suggest you work out your issues through counselling, because 'nothing good comes of separation'. (Of course, they mean nothing good financially, and the flip side to that is that without happiness, nothing good happens!) Counsellors may also try to facilitate the parties to work out their differences, again because separation is hard and causes strain, stress, and anxiety, which is only exacerbated when children are involved.

If there is no other way — which is likely if you are holding this book — then there are some difficult conversations ahead. Have you discussed separation seriously with your partner? Are you in agreement? Whatever stage you are at in your separation process, some counselling or other professional advice might help, even just to establish a means of communicating productively.

In the interests of communicating effectively, how would you have felt if your former partner had sat down with you and said, 'I'd like to have an open and honest conversation'? You probably would have paid attention and even have been open to a sensible discussion, recognising that this is a courageous action for them to take. This type of communication will be referred to in this book as 'wise adult' behaviour. We are not born wise, and it is hard to behave wisely in stressful situations. Approaching every communication as a 'wise adult' opens up positive opportunities for issues to be discussed and resolved.

Creating a framework within which to have a difficult conversation enables the other person to rise up to the wise adult level, whoever you are talking to. It could be a child or your former partner, other family members, friends. You can use this framework in any situation. Learning how to be the best possible 'wise adult' you can is a life skill well worth learning.

A key component of being a wise adult is being assertive and staying assertive. Stating your needs, wants, or feelings in an honest, direct, appropriate, and sensitive way contributes to calm, two-way conversations where feelings are accurately and sensitively presented in a way which invites productive dialogue and resolution of issues.

CHILDREN COME FIRST

SO HOW DO you tell your children you are separating from their other parent? As is usually the case, the truth is best. The New Zealand Law Society website suggests, 'Dad/Mum and I have agreed not to live together. We both love you and you will be able to spend lots of time with each of us.' Clear and honest. If you tell them together, use your 'wise adult' skills. Not attributing blame will encourage the children to feel more secure and able to deal with the situation. They don't need to be involved in who's right and who's wrong, just that things are different now, and it will still work.

Children of all ages are affected deeply when the family unit breaks down. Where the children are still dependent, there is plenty of help available. You can find out about counselling services through the Citizens Advice Bureau, your lawyer, or school.

Children look to you to signpost how they should behave, so your attitude is pivotal in how your children cope with separation. Regardless of your feelings, your children need your love, care, and attention; and they need to be actively encouraged to maintain their relationship with their other parent.

Broad research around the topic, combined with conversations and personal experience, suggests children need you to give them the time and space to tell you what they feel. Critically for children, rather than explaining or trying to correct what you see as a misinterpretation, actively listen, mirror what you hear, and empathise. That way, when they hear you validating how they feel, they will know you have really heard and understood their issues. You may be surprised at the calming influence this has.

As hard as it might be, encourage them to love and respect both parents, holding back from angry communications with your former partner or negative comments about them in front of the children. Children will take sides if you encourage them to, or if they are exposed to situations where they feel one parent is being treated badly.

When coming to a co-parenting arrangement, if they are old enough, it can help children to adapt if they are involved in future plans. That said, it is of course easiest for the children if their lives change as little as possible.

In day-to-day management of the family, there may need to be some ground rules around how you will communicate what the arrangements are, and how important it is to stick to the arrangement, avoiding the potential for anger and frustration. It's understandable that you may want less communication with your former partner but leaving it to the children to make arrangements puts an unnecessary burden on them. If you are not the main caregiver, try to establish or maintain regular contact with your children and participate in their lives as much as you can — they do need you too.

It's common sense not to further harm the fragile relationship with your former partner by priming the children to cause trouble. Things will go better for everyone if you show respect in your co-parenting arrangement — only go into their home if you are invited; and allow your children to spend as much time as they need with their other parent. While you may be desperate to know what's going on inside (and what they have spent their money on), try not to pry!

However you think things are going for your children, reassure them frequently that it's not their fault, you still love them, and separation isn't unusual. They will need plenty of affection from you, and for you to listen to how they feel. You can't change the pain they feel, but you can support them.

Ideally you will come to an agreement with your former partner about the care of the children, using a counsellor or other facilitator if necessary, rather than referring to the Family Court. You will hear many times that the needs of the children are paramount.

In real life — the challenges of young children

> Rob and I were a good parenting team, together. I was the more pragmatic one, organising and running the household, but also creating space for him outside of his busy and stressful work life to have fun with our daughter. We had met in our early 30s, both having been through long relationships in the past. We had both travelled widely and I had had a successful sporting career. Rob was building a professional practice.
>
> After 12 years together, we separated. Our daughter Ruby was nine. I think Rob just missed his freedom, and I gave him a full year to get that out of his system, taking sole care of our daughter. Looking back, maybe I just didn't trust him to provide the practicalities of a nine-year-old's life, but I admit also I was relieved not to have to deal with him and his complicated personality.
>
> It was a confusing time as I grappled with single mum-hood. I found it hard to satisfy Ruby's need for fun alongside all the other factors weighing on my mind around my career, money, and where I would live once the family home was sold. I remember us sitting in silence some mealtimes, each lost in this new reality and what it meant.
>
> Rob and I did try to protect Ruby from the disruption as much as possible, and at nine she didn't fully understand what separation meant. I

was doing my best, but she missed her dad. They have similar personalities and that made it harder for her.

By the time Rob had worked through his need for 'freedom' I was desperate for some space of my own and we eventually agreed to a 'week on, week off' arrangement with Ruby travelling between our houses. This worked well for me and I know Rob enjoyed reconnecting with Ruby, indulging her with a lifestyle I had no chance of providing her. Private schools, a pony, and weekends in Fiji made my camping on the Coromandel rather substandard. However, I was enjoying a social life again; I joined a sports club, met new people (including men), and just had some fun.

It wasn't a huge surprise to me when Ruby announced, at 12, that she wanted to live full time with Rob. It was a smart choice really, for her, and I remember thinking it would be good for their relationship and, having not had much input up to that point, it was sort of his turn. While it was hard to let her go, I never felt jealous or fearful that I would lose Ruby. In the next few years Ruby met several of Rob's girlfriends, counselled him when the relationships failed, cleaned house, cooked meals, and organised him.

Ruby became interested in sport at high school and that was my opening into her world. We strongly connected and I believe she started to understand me through that connection. I like to think she realised that to balance out her development, she needed me.

We went through some tough times together, Ruby and me. It has taken a long time, but we have a strong relationship now. For her to recognise the value I offered needed a catalyst, and that was fending for herself financially and being in her own good relationship.

It would be foolish to think you can parent better alone. You can do well, but it's not the same. Ruby is now 26, and I'm so proud of her and all she has been through and achieved. The tough times were worth it.

Adult children

There are also hard conversations to be had with your adult children. How will they react? Even adult children have a hard time adjusting to separation, and we are likely to have exposed adult children to more criticism of the other parent and allowed them to witness more negativity in the relationship in the form of anger or coldness than we would have if they were younger. While they are adults and will have adult questions for you, don't necessarily expect adult reactions. The parent-child dynamic never really goes away and this extreme change to how they imagined their family to look in the future will be traumatic.

In real life — experiences of an adult child

> My parents ended their long, toxic relationship when I was in my early 20s. I had always had a close relationship with my mother, sharing confidences while she shared complaints about Dad, but otherwise she kept her feelings very much to herself.
>
> I never witnessed warmth or romantic love between my parents. I could see that Mum wanted this, but their relationship had been too hostile for that to be possible. There was a lot of anger in the relationship and they both tolerated terrible behaviour from each other. Mum in particular seemed to encourage me to tolerate the same in my life. Despite all this, we did still manage to have some sense of family identity, we shared a sense of humour and had family rituals, and I have some happy memories of my childhood.
>
> Before it ended, I knew Mum wanted to leave. I was supportive, but when she told me she had ended the relationship, I felt numb. Shocked. Worried about Dad and confused about what it meant logistically. I can barely remember this period, though it was only a few years ago. It heralded the beginning of an incredibly strange phase of my life, which I could never have anticipated.

I was 21 and frankly already incredibly fucked up by the problematic dynamic within which I had grown up. I had no knowledge of how to establish emotional boundaries or allow myself to feel normal emotions.

Both my parents leaned on me for emotional support after the break-up, but in different ways. Dad was incredibly hurt and would cry all the time. I thought he might kill himself and it would be my fault. Mum began sharing details of her new experiences with dating and sex with me, though I frequently asked her not to. It was horrific. She changed everything about herself — her dress sense, her friendships, the food she cooked, her social behaviour, her way of speaking.

I had gained a new boundary-irreverent 'friend' and lost the person who would normally have helped me deal with such a person. I know she was just trying to be a person in her own right and was intensely vulnerable. Our relationship was understandably tested.

The financial aspect of the separation was a source of major anxiety for me and my sisters. Both our parents felt somehow ruined, and we all knew too much about the huge legal fees and assets they had shared and were fighting over. While eager to know how (or even that) things were progressing, even adult children don't need detail. I set some boundaries of my own about this, asking them not to tell me unless I asked for an update. That was helpful.

Out the other side, for me:

I recently acquired a new boyfriend who drove 90 minutes to see me after work. A member of the family commented, 'That's a long way to drive,' and mum exclaimed, 'Worth it though!' That meant a lot to me. I know she has always loved me, but suggesting I was worth a lot of effort made me realise how far she has also come, and what a journey she has been on.

It is impossible to teach a small, growing human to respect themselves when you are allowing somebody to treat you without respect. Looking back, I am glad such a troubled relationship has ended, and Mum has found self-respect. This has allowed me to develop greater respect for myself, understanding that what I grew up witnessing was not good enough.

In real life — a dad's life

I thought that once we separated, my relationship with my two boys would improve. It seemed likely that the strains of the failing relationship had spilled over to make all relationships within the family difficult at that time. But I was wrong.

My late-teen children both refused to talk with me about the break-up and they broke off most contact with me subsequently. I've tried repeatedly to talk to them and understand what lies behind this, but so far, they both refuse to open up and discuss what the real problem is.

There is not much left for me to do other than wait and continue living my life.

WHERE WILL YOU LIVE?

THE ISSUE of where to live, who moves out and who stays in the family home, are common to most relationship break-ups. It is normal for separated couples to need space to work through their grief and to come to terms with their new situation and would do anything not to be in the same house if at all possible.

As a single person with or without dependent children, the cost of running the family home may be too high and a more cost-effective option may need to be found. Having said that, causing as little disruption to any dependent children must be factored in, for example, avoiding changes to schooling and friendships means staying in the general area.

One of the financial implications of separation is that, for most couples, two dwellings are needed which means an added burden on relationship funds. If it doesn't make sense for either party to keep the home, it can be sold, and more affordable options found.

In the immediate aftermath of separation, finding a space for a single person is quite different to housing a family. Are there friends or family with space to spare to get through the first few months? Is there reasonably priced rental accommodation available? If the children are moving too, it needs to be somewhere relatively stable to avoid additional change.

As with all aspects of separation, a lot depends on your financial situation. There is government assistance available to help with housing costs, and advice on this can be found by contacting the Citizens Advice Bureau.

In real life — the other housing crisis

> *We were together for eight years, I thought happily, but something changed with the birth of our baby one year ago. We both work full time in average-earning jobs. We could never afford to buy a house on our incomes, but my wife's family agreed to help out, buying half of the house we live in through their family trust. My wife and I own the remaining half, but we have a substantial mortgage.*
>
> *You can see where this is leading — if we separate, my wife has her family trust's contribution AND her quarter of our house, effectively all but one-quarter of the property value. I am left with one-*

quarter of this average house, and we both still have to repay the mortgage.

Neither of us can afford to buy the other out because of the mortgage; and neither of us can afford to buy a house on our own. Our incomes separately are not enough to buy or rent two places, both of which need to be suitable to raise a baby.

We agree we want to co-parent, so for the meantime we have no realistic choice but to live together, separately. It's increasingly difficult to focus on work with these financial problems compounding the emotional issues we are facing while staying upbeat and attentive to our baby. We just don't know what to do.

ARE PETS CHILDREN?

WHATEVER YOU MAY FEEL about them, pets are not children. According to the law in New Zealand they are 'family chattels'. Property. They are subject to the division of property rules outlined in the legal section below. As you would expect, however, the primary concern issue is the welfare of the pets.

Sharing family pets requires the same type of communications as making arrangements for children, with picking up and dropping off, ensuring the pet's needs are met in both locations. Think about the pet when making these decisions and be as flexible as possible with your former partner.

In real life — I raised him!

> *Having spent 12 years walking, feeding, and caring for their family dog through injuries and*

ailments, Suzy felt it only fair that she should continue to care for Frank, a Labrador. He should live with her — right? 'He's basically my fourth child!' Her husband, Marcus, disagreed, claiming Frank needed him!

Frank didn't enjoy the best of health, needing frequent medication and vet visits. Initially Suzy and Marcus agreed to share custody, a week each. Like with children, this required negotiating a handover time and place, and for two of everything to be on hand — medication, his comfy bed.

'After a few months, Frank twigged that this wasn't a short-term fun thing,' says Suzy. 'He began to show signs of severe distress — refusing to eat and take his medication and needing to be taken outside to the garden several times in the night for his ablutions!' Suzy saw the writing on the wall — Frank just wasn't happy with all the swapping around. It was too confusing and unsettling. She decided to allow Marcus full 'custody' of Frank, in his best interests.

'It just wasn't fair to Frank to fight over him, and I decided this was one battle I could walk away from.' While she misses Frank's company around the house, Suzy acknowledges one small advantage to not having him constantly in her life, and that is that she has been able to *experience greater freedom. Is Suzy keen to get another dog? 'Maybe in a few years. I think to be a good pet owner you need stability, and I just don't have that yet.'*

PART 2
AIMING FOR EMOTIONAL REGULATION

An enormous aspect of any separation is managing emotions. Each party to the relationship — and others affected by the break-up — will have difficult emotions to cope with.

ARE YOU COPING?

THE STRONG EMOTIONS evoked by a break-up will likely make you feel vulnerable — which may be a new feeling. Some ways to cope with these feelings:

- Accept support from friends and family, but remember they are not mind-readers so if you need help, ask for it.
- Talking through your new situation with a friend or adviser helps to clarify not only how you feel but what you want out of your settlement.
- Be honest with trusted friends about what's going on for you.
- Positively pay attention to your health — food, exercise, and drug and alcohol intake.
- You are going through a lot — it's not only okay, but essential, to grieve for your past relationship.
- Get professional help if you feel you're losing the battle (your GP is a good place to start, and there

are social support agencies available to advise also).
- Talking to people who are in a similar position to you will really help — it can even be a way to make new friendships through shared experiences.

GRIEVING WHAT YOU HAVE LOST

AN IMPORTANT ASPECT of relationships falling apart is grief. While similar to when a person dies, in this case the person is not dead, but the loss still causes immense upheaval and heartache. Unlike death, with a separation the person leaving has done so voluntarily.

They will have worked through many of the stages of grief prior to separation, but the person who was left is starting from scratch. Here we talk through the various stages of grief, starting from the point of view of the person who was left. The stages are not linear, and don't follow any schedule, so how you grieve (and how long you grieve) will be different to someone else.

Denial is a defence mechanism. It buys you time and numbs the intensity of your feelings. As with every stage, it can last seconds, minutes, days, or months.

'You don't mean that.' 'You're just upset.'

This is closely aligned with *pain and guilt*, where you may feel the loss is unbearable but that you played a part in the decision.

'How could she/he?' 'How did I mess this up?'

Anger hides pain and intense emotions and will most likely be directed at the one who has caused the pain. In a break-up, anger could be presented as bitterness or resentment rather than fury, but fury is also a legitimate way to feel anger! This stage can also be expressed as revenge fantasies.

'I hate him/her.' 'I'm going to make sure everyone knows what she/he has done to me.'

Bargaining to regain control or to mitigate the effects of the separation postpones the sadness, confusion and hurt which will inevitably follow. Thoughts tend to follow the 'what if' or 'if only' pattern.

'What if we start over?' 'If only I had paid more attention, it would never have come to this.'

Depression is a more inward-looking stage. You face your emotions and work through them. Choosing to isolate from others is common, allowing you the space to comprehend and cope with the loss. It can be overwhelming and confusing and is often the stage where you get stuck. If that happens to you, speak to a counsellor to work through this period.

'What's the point?' 'I'll never have another relationship, I'm a failure.'

Acceptance simply means coming to terms with the loss and what it means for your life now. While you may continue to experience bad days, your perspective on the separation may change unexpectedly, and through acceptance comes constructive understanding and even hope.

'*I really don't miss the tension.*' '*I want to learn from my mistakes and sort out what went wrong in the relationship.*'

The stages for the person leaving might be represented by statements such as '*I can't believe I'm going to do this*' (denial), '*I've ignored my feelings in this relationship*' (pain), '*How dare she/he behave in such a way that it's come to this*' (anger), '*I can't wait to ...*' (acceptance and hope). Distancing from the relationship while still in it is a way to evaluate and work through how life will be after it ends. Depression can come at any stage in the process for the person who leaves as they consider the enormity of what is to come, or the reality.

Talking through any of the stages of grief with a close, trusted friend is recommended, but consider engaging a professional should that become necessary. It is a very personal process and can take a very long time — even years — to work through all the feelings and changes.

GETTING HELP — COACHING AND COUNSELLING

RELATIONSHIP BREAK-UPS ARE STRESSFUL. That stress may be caused by any number of emotions, particular to your situation. Regardless of whether you left or were left, both of your lives have been turned upside down and there will be a lot of changes — living arrangements, finances, children, property division, maybe even careers.

The issue of how each person in the relationship sees their contribution to the break-up can be addressed in counselling. Understanding your role in the breakdown of your relationship is an important aspect of moving forward in your life, especially if entering a new relationship. If your budget doesn't include counselling, there are options available which can provide you with counselling, but at limited cost to you. Many larger employers offer an 'Employee Assistance Programme' (EAP). The objective is to address personal needs, privately, outside the workplace. Another option is to speak to a Citizens Advice Bureau for information on community help in your area.

Making decisions while in emotional turmoil is not recommended, but decisions are forced on you while you are in this state. A counsellor or other trained professional will help you manage your emotions and guide you to explore alternatives and make rational decisions, with the aim of increasing your self-awareness and enabling you to grow with the hindsight of your difficult break-up situation. They can provide a neutral space where you can openly talk, either together or separately, without blame and accusations.

The issues to deal with are wide ranging and vary greatly between individuals. Some will be grieving or angry, feeling betrayal and loss, recovering from abuse, or regaining the ability to trust in future relationships. Others will feel guilty over their part in the break-up, or what they did or didn't do to make the relationship work.

A key ingredient in counselling is trust. It simply won't work if one party is hiding something or is unwilling to open up completely or is even saying one thing and doing another. Counselling only works if both parties agree and the situation is balanced, fair, and safe. When the balance shifts, trust is lost, so another system may need to be used to create a structure within which to negotiate. The legal system does this, albeit a little heavy-handedly.

It's relatively common for one person in the relationship to be keen to attend counselling, but the other person to be resistant. The resistance could be from fear that the counselling may be manipulated by their partner, they could consider themselves weaker at talking about feelings, or it could be that they are not motivated to fix the problems. They should be encouraged to speak to someone, alone. Counselling is still worthwhile, even if only one of the couple attends.

There are two roadblocks in separations, both of which usually require outside help to resolve — children and money. Disputes about children can often be resolved with counselling together, always with the objective of creating the fairest deal possible for the sake of the children. If finances can't be resolved amicably, you are likely to need legal advice.

Amicable separation

If you are separating amicably, using a relationship counsellor to facilitate could be a pathway worth exploring. They will guide you to control your emotions and to acknowledge and address the pain you feel, encouraging you to be honest about your feelings and compassionate towards your former partner. You will still feel pain, but it will be the 'clean' pain of speaking honestly rather than the 'dirty' pain of an unhappy relationship where the other person is being hurt. Clean pain is unavoidable, dirty pain is unnecessary.

Acrimonious separation

If your separation is not amicable, at least one person in the relationship will feel angry and resentful, even hurt, betrayed, or abandoned. They may be shocked; they may also believe the relationship could be salvaged and be willing to work hard to fix it.

The party who made the final decision to end things may feel relieved that it's all out in the open and that action is being taken. While they will likely have processed a lot in the time leading up to the break-up, there will still be a lot of change in the coming months and years.

Once over the initial shock, the party who was left may also feel relieved that the tension within the relationship is no longer present in their daily life. There will be many factors to come to terms with, and it will take time.

As your relationship broke down you may have sought advice and counselling either alone or together. Good for you. If not, simply having the break-up conversation with your partner in a 'wise adult' manner may present an opportunity for you to seek counselling to work through separation issues. Generally speaking, if one party in a relationship is unhappy enough to consider ending it, there is something wrong and something to talk about.

In real life — coaching leads to decisions

It took Jonah years to get to the point where he seriously considered leaving his partner, Judith. At 49 he was very unhappy. 'I was gaining weight through stress eating and generally not looking after myself. I hadn't talked to anyone about it, but I reckon it was pretty obvious what was going on: I just wanted Judith gone.'

One of Jonah's friends put him in touch with a coach. They asked him three questions which helped him to make a decision. The questions Jonah's coach asked were specifically targeted at his personal situation. The questions were:

* If Judith were diagnosed with a life-threatening illness, would you care for her?

* If Judith suggested we take a year off work to travel, would you want to do that with her?

* If you could just walk away from everything — your lifestyle, sell your home, your work — and start afresh somewhere new, would you want to do that with Judith?

Jonah's reaction was momentous. Answering 'no' to these three questions meant 'I wanted the lifestyle but not the person', and that made it easier for him to start thinking about what would come next. Over the next several months Jonah mulled over what this meant for his future, and he started processing the many changes which would be necessary.

'I was walking away from the family unit. Walking away from some very old joint friends and Judith's extended family. Not to mention the impact on my children and Judith — how would they cope?'

Jonah continues, 'Have I had moments of doubt or regret over my decision? No. I had really reached a tipping point and if I had said "yes" to remaining in the relationship, I would have been saying "no" to what could only be a happier future, even if I was alone.'

PART 3
COMMUNICATING

Looking back, things could always have gone better. The way we communicate is paramount and often where we come unstuck. In this section we will address the various relationships outside your nuclear family which you will be managing in the months and years to come.

COMMUNICATING BETTER WITH YOUR FORMER PARTNER

COMMUNICATION with your former partner post separation will take place on a new footing. Old methods of communication which may have contributed to your break-up need to be replaced. It's very common to get stuck in an unhealthy cycle of communication when a relationship is in trouble, with loss of trust and a breakdown in honest communication, resulting in anger and blame. Avoiding this happening in future relationships is essential and is discussed later in this book, but for now we will focus on creating a new framework for communication with your former partner.

Ideally the new form of communication will be courteous yet functional, leaving out accusations and recriminations. Developing a line of communication which works for you both is essential, especially if children are involved.

It cannot be stressed enough how carefully emails and texts must be drafted. What is written and sent is not always what is received by the reader. While you might feel angry or resentful, don't let your communication descend into acrimony (it's really not easy, so good luck!). A good trick is to read what has been written, through the eyes of the recipient, removing any barbed comments or emotional language which detract from the message.

Integrity is a good word to use when bursting into print whether in emails or on social media, so take a moment to consider the impact on your former partner or others when drafting your email or post. If you receive an email or see a post intended to be hurtful to you, try not to engage.

When moving on to the legal side of your separation, it's worth noting that disagreement over division of assets can be a continuation of disagreements during the relationship. Continuing to fight keeps the old relationship issues alive, costs money, and does nothing for your future happiness. If you can, communicate just on the issues at hand with your former partner and focus on the future, keeping negative comments and emotions from creeping into emails between you.

Your communications with your former partner can become evidence should your separation make it to court, so keep them on point. Choosing your words carefully will come across as more credible than angry outbursts or ignoring communications. Sometimes it's best to write what you want to say, leave it for an hour, then come back and remove the emotion before hitting send.

In real life — on reflection

> *Looking back, Sarah thinks things could have gone better. She knew her relationship had been unfulfilling for both her and her long-term partner Lucy for several years prior to separation, but Sarah didn't communicate that — in words — to Lucy. Communication in the relationship generally had become almost non-existent. 'Instead of talking, I would lash out with a cutting personal comment which was met with sullen silence,' recalls Sarah.*
>
> *In the last few months of the relationship, Sarah describes herself as having become distant and observant, 'judging Lucy to assess whether I would stay or leave'. She eventually resolved to leave following another awful holiday which they bickered their way through. During yet another argument the night before, Lucy suggested separation. 'This was by no means the first time this had come up,' says Sarah. 'I had a very restless night, and the next morning I said I would like to separate.'*
>
> *To Sarah's astonishment, Lucy was shocked. Sarah's decision was — to Lucy — out of the blue,*

leaving her no opportunity to try to fix things. Lucy suggested they go to counselling, but Sarah had made up her mind. As Sarah saw it, there was no point.

In hindsight, however difficult it would have been for Sarah, she believes counselling would have given Lucy greater insight into how Sarah had arrived at her decision, and it would have given Lucy an opportunity to say what she needed to. It would have helped her to arrive at the same point Sarah was at.

Sarah believes the result was a greater level of animosity towards her, and a longer road to financial settlement.

In real life — learning about myself through counselling

> *My partner and I started counselling after a crisis in our relationship more than five years before we separated.*
>
> *With the benefit of hindsight, I can see that my agreement to attend counselling was more of a penance to bear, almost a punishment for my failings and actions than a genuine grasp for change. I think that deep down I had already decided that I wanted to leave the relationship, weakening my commitment to creating change. Perhaps I sabotaged the process*

as I was initially committed to not working toward a rapprochement. Rather, I was looking for a way back to 'an easy life'; even a return to mediocrity looked better than the situation we were in.

However, I do not view the many counselling sessions as a waste. The counsellors we saw (together or separately) approached the situation with an open mind and the goal of helping us to decide our future instead of pushing us together (or apart). Overall, I learned a lot about myself, my relationships and the many factors that influence them, including the predispositions we bring because of our upbringing and life experiences.

I was not good at communicating my emotions. That made many of the sessions angst-ridden and stressful, and exposed my failings, especially when compared to my partner's more savvy skills. This made the feeling of penance all the more intense. Slowly I improved my understanding, and I became more aware of my needs and my rights in the relationship.

I learned how to communicate more effectively, and to speak up when I didn't feel my needs were being considered. I recognise now that relationships are all about benefits and sacrifices, and a true partnership takes account of all parties in the partnership. Understanding this has allowed me to let go of a lot of the guilt I felt at the failure of my past relationship.

Counselling didn't save our relationship, but it did make me a better person and contributed positively toward how I approached future relationships.

PEOPLE OTHER THAN YOUR FORMER PARTNER AND YOUR CHILDREN

GIVEN how common relationship breakdowns are, it's somewhat surprising that people outside the relationship often don't know how to behave. Some friends will skirt around the topic, avoid you altogether, or ask deeply personal questions which you really don't want to answer. Even worse, they may tell you what to do or how you should behave, or what you have done wrong. Relationship breakdowns can also, however, be an opportunity for friends to share their own experiences and can build deeper relationships.

Having a pre-prepared 'speech' makes answering difficult questions easier and has the added advantage of ensuring everyone is on the same page. Don't forget you are in charge of this conversation — you have no obligation to divulge any information you don't feel comfortable relating. Signalling to friends and family what you need them to do helps to maintain the relationship into the future.

It is best to simply be honest. People will gossip and share details, whether you like it or not. It can be liberating to be honest and open about your separation.

In real life — nosy neighbours

> *Several months after separating from her husband, Rose walked into a local bar to have a glass of wine with an old friend. She was stopped by a couple she had seen around the neighbourhood over the years, sometimes in the company of her former husband. 'We were just distant acquaintances, not even friends, and I hadn't seen them since separating from my ex.'*
>
> *After a quick hello and a very personal comment on her appearance, Rose was confronted with the question, 'Have you settled financially yet?' More than a little taken aback, she answered with the truth, which, she claims was 'my first mistake'. It opened the door to further, even more searching questions. The neighbourhood acquaintances concluded their exchange with the statement, 'He really loved you, you know.' Actually, says Rose, 'No, he didn't, and how could these strangers possibly have that insight!'*
>
> *Rose didn't make that mistake again. 'I consciously switch into marketing mode when accosted by*

people just looking for an update, just to avoid that feeling of being public property.'

Shared friends

Inevitably friendships change and allegiances shift in a relationship split. It's hard for some people to maintain friendships with both parties, so they will naturally gravitate to one or other of you or your former partner. It's not always related to the origin of the friendship, and it's not always apparent why these decisions are made.

You may imagine your former partner has said hurtful things about you to friends of the relationship, but you have no control over this, and it may be best to just rise above rather than trying to justify your position or correct misapprehensions.

Some old friends will simply not make contact, often because they simply don't know how to communicate how they feel. Some secure couples seem to think separation is contagious and may not include you in future social gatherings! Strange but true. This could be because it reflects an insecurity of their own rather than a reflection on you, so try to be empathetic, even though it may be hurtful.

Be prepared to let former friends go. You may be surprised months or even years down the track that you reconnect in different, more mature, ways.

In real life — what is a friend?

> *Following the end of my relationship, it was obvious most of our joint friends had no idea there had been anything wrong. A consequence of this was that I was invited to many 'fact finding' or — worse — 'fact sharing' lunches or drinks, but once the gossip was out, they disappeared. Some of these people had been very good friends.*
>
> *I recall being invited to one such lunch a few months after I separated. It became apparent the express purpose was to tell me my former partner was in a new relationship. Maybe they needed to witness my reaction. I'll never know.*
>
> *This has been a big lesson for me — I may have been that person in the past. Now, I make a point to be inclusive and kind to people going down this awful path, or to any of my friends who may be lonely or alone, and to actively seek their company.*

Family other than children

Both parties in a relationship have a relationship with the other's parents, siblings, and wider family members. If they have been in the family for many years, significant history has been established and strong relationships formed. Rather than stepping away from your former partner, those relationships may need to be realigned or altered to accommodate the separation. By including them in family news they have the opportunity to continue to have an active role in the family, taking account of the new boundaries, but only if they want it.

In real life — I thought you were my family

> Maria had no family of her own, so she adopted her former husband's extended family. She had a great relationship with her parents-in-law, and her husband's siblings, nieces, and nephews. Her children were close to their cousins, growing up in the same neighbourhood and attending the same schools. 'It never occurred to me that separation would result in me losing my connection with Greg's family,' says Maria. 'Having supported my husband in his work all our married life, I have had jobs but no proper career of my own, focusing instead on family. Greg's extended family were present for all of the years I was with Greg.'
>
> On separation, Maria was assured by various members of Greg's family that they would continue to include her in family events — birthdays, Christmases, weddings — and that they would continue to 'keep her in the loop, since Greg was never particularly good at keeping up with family goings on.'
>
> Actions speak louder than words, however, and Maria found herself left out of everything. When

her sister-in-law got engaged, she heard nothing. When her niece graduated, nothing. And on it went. When Maria challenged her brother-in-law, he simply said 'blood is thicker than water'.

Maria is hopeful that once she has a financial settlement with her former husband, things might change. 'I really hope that we can get back to a different "normal" once this is over, if not for me then for my kids.'

In real life — are they still family?

> When I split from my wife five years ago, my ex-wife retained fairly regular contact with my extended family. It feels a little weird that she has these relationships given that I see very little of her. It can lead to occasional social functions that I am not invited to, but she is! Even though I don't like it much, I can't really begrudge her continuing those relationships. She is the mother of my kids and was part of my family for many years.

CLOSING THE DOOR ON ABUSIVE OR CONTROLLING BEHAVIOUR

THANKFULLY, there is a lot of information on the internet about power and control in relationships. Women's Refuge in New Zealand claims the stress caused by the exertion of power and control is most frequently experienced by women. Through having less power, particularly financially, women are trapped in the relationship. If the car needs to be replaced but it is registered in the former partner's name, for example, it gives them the opportunity to exercise financial control.

The person who has been treated badly is usually the most vulnerable. It takes a lot of courage for a victim of abuse to leave the relationship, and this person is often facing decisions on matters they have never had to think about before, or they may have lost confidence through the abuse. It's very frightening to be striking out alone, ill equipped.

It is widely recognised that abusive behaviour is gendered, and it's usually kept hidden from the public eye. Here in New Zealand, we have a shockingly high incidence of abuse. Abusive behaviour within the relationship is often continued after the relationship has ended. If you or your partner engaged in any form of bad behaviour, this is the time to address it.

Communication in the future needs to be clear and professional, with the objective of not allowing the opportunity for abuse to arise. As is discussed elsewhere, try to remember this when writing or responding to not-so-professional messages.

Abusive behaviour is not limited to physical violence and is not necessarily related to socioeconomic status. Again, mostly from the Women's Refuge website, abusive behaviour can take many forms. These include:

- emotional or psychological abuse (threatening to harm you or the children, belittling, damaging property, stalking, isolating from friends and family)
- financial or economic abuse (withholding funds, demanding evidence of expenditure, making all financial decisions)
- technical abuse (taking advantage of your shared accounts or knowledge of passwords to cause mischief)
- physical abuse (any physical act causing injury)
- sexual abuse (harassing, degrading, forcing to have sex)

- personality issues such as narcissism, which may be exacerbated by the particular dynamics of your relationship.

It is very difficult to leave an abusive relationship, so if you are reading this having done so, well done. Delving further into these issues is beyond the scope of this book, but there is information and help available online, or through your lawyer, GP, or counsellor.

PART 4
WHAT NOW? REACHING AGREEMENT

Having found somewhere to live, having had those tricky conversations, and are adjusting to your new situation, it's time to address the formal part of your separation.

What is the most appropriate path for you and your former partner? You can have more than one. If using a friend or counsellor to help sort out matters doesn't work, then you might need a lawyer. If you don't trust your former partner, you need a lawyer right away, but that doesn't mean you can't eventually come to a resolution through direct negotiation once you understand all the issues. This section addresses what the options are.

RESOLVING YOUR DISPUTE

UNLESS YOU ARE A LAWYER, law is pretty dry. It's also complex and hard to navigate without training and experience. This outline of the law in New Zealand will hopefully enable you to enter the process eyes open and aware of the challenges ahead.

Please be aware it is a guide only, and you should consult a lawyer or visit a Community Law Centre or Citizens Advice Bureau for guidance on the law as it relates to your case.

Resolution options

There are several methods to consider when resolving your financial separation. What you choose will largely depend on the relationship between the parties involved, and their frame of mind. This section outlines the various options, in order of outside involvement and cost —

negotiation, assisted negotiation, collaborative law, mediation, arbitration, court, and Family Dispute Resolution. The Family Dispute Resolution service provided by the Family Court in New Zealand is included at the end of this section because it stands alone, not because of its cost.

In New Zealand, the Property (Relationships) Act 1976 is the law that governs how property is to be divided after separation, and applies to married, civil union, or de facto relationships. Any relationship where the parties have been living together for more than three years falls within the ambit of the Act which means that, should the relationship fail, any assets will be divided according to that Act.

There are a couple of exceptions. The first is a marriage of short duration, defined as a marriage of less than three years. This is not the same as simply living together for less than three years where there are no legal grounds for sharing assets. The law on this point is explained further in the legal section.

Another exception is where the parties have a property-sharing agreement — also called a Contracting Out Agreement or pre-nuptial agreement — in place. Again, this will be explained further in the legal section. A Contracting Out Agreement will have been negotiated by the parties at some early point in their relationship and sets out the terms for division of property in the event that the relationship breaks down, effectively agreeing not to be bound by the Property (Relationships) Act.

Contracting Out Agreements are also talked about in the section dealing with new relationships because they offer protection in the event of another relationship breaking down.

What you 'want' and what you 'need' from your settlement may be quite different things, and while it's very difficult to do so in an emotional state, think as realistically as possible about your expectations. This is especially hard in the early stages of separation.

Negotiation with your partner directly

If your separation is amicable, or there is little property and no other factors to consider, a simple negotiation between the parties may be possible. This straightforward division of property must be recorded in writing and signed off by each party's lawyer. The lawyer must certify that they have discussed the effect and implications of the agreement with you. This is not the straightforward matter you might imagine because to do that there needs to be full disclosure and agreed values.

With any separation it's always worth attempting direct negotiation. Even in the course of a protracted legal negotiation, a direct discussion between the parties **can** help to move things along. If, however, you are not comfortable doing this, or it causes an unreasonable or unacceptable amount of stress, stop, and communicate through your lawyer or another trusted adviser.

Assisted negotiation

It is also possible to negotiate with the assistance of a third party. That could be a trusted mutual friend, or a counsellor. Putting a buffer between the parties can encourage more respectful dialogue, creating a slightly more formal forum than a simple exchange with your former partner.

As with direct negotiation, the resulting agreement on the division of assets needs to be in writing and each party needs to have independent legal advice, as set out in the section above.

Collaborative law

Originating in the US, 'collaborative law' is a separate and recognised dispute resolution process which removes the threat of court from the discussion, while still using lawyers and professional specialists to advise and guide through the separation process. Removing court takes away the uncertainty of a third party — a judge — making decisions for you and your family. You will begin by signing an agreement committing you and your former partner to the process of working together. You will agree to considering issues which are important to each party and the family, with the objective of arriving at a result which works for your particular situation in an amicable way.

Facts and information are disclosed, and advisers guide their clients using a forward-thinking problem-solving approach involving exchanges of information and face-to-face meetings. It is more cost effective than court, and more efficient than negotiating by exchanges of letters between lawyers. Disputes, by their nature, involve conflict and stress, and this process can relieve some of that by allowing the personal issues of each party to be heard and managed in a supportive manner.

Practitioners of collaborative law are usually lawyers with additional training in this area of dispute resolution. In the unlikely event that no resolution is reached, the practitioner representing you cannot represent you in future litigation. Many lawyers will say they work collaboratively — and many do — but 'collaborative practice' is a separate area of training, so if you are interested in this and your lawyer says they work collaboratively, satisfy yourself that they have the appropriate qualifications.

This sounds like a great avenue to pursue, but it's only possible if both parties agree to the process and participate in every way, including providing honest and full information about financial and other matters. It's not a 'soft option', but a serious alternative dispute resolution process.

Mediation

This is a dispute resolution process where an independent person — a mediator — is appointed to assist the parties to reach agreement to resolve their disputes. There is no 'court' involved, but this process does not remove the possibility of legal proceedings being issued should the mediation not result in an agreement. If no agreement is reached, the process has no bearing on future legal proceedings.

Everything discussed at mediation is conditional and 'privileged' (meaning private) and as such cannot be referred to in any subsequent litigation.

It is usual for the parties to have received legal advice in advance of the mediation, and facts and other information will have been collated and a strategy worked out. In a mediation, the lawyers and the parties can all be involved in presenting the case. The mediator's job is to facilitate communication, direct the focus on the real issues, and help to develop options which aid agreement. They have no power to impose or enforce any decision or make a judgment.

It is the responsibility of the lawyers in a mediation to advise their client of their legal entitlements and the costs associated, and your lawyer will challenge the other side's lawyer if they don't agree with a point of law. When agreement is achieved, the lawyers will document it and will explain to their client the effect and extent of the agreement. Your lawyer is required to sign the agreement to demonstrate that they have carried out this duty.

A mediation can be held at any point, at the request of either party. A mediator is selected and agreed, and a mutually agreeable date set. There is significant preparation for a mediation, as with a court case — valuations of assets by registered valuers, financial evidence provided by accounting experts, legal analysis of your case and relevant case law, and armed with all that you should have an idea of the result you realistically believe you can achieve.

With legal fees preparing for the mediation then attending the mediation, plus the mediator's fee, the cost is not insignificant. If successful, however, it will be substantially less than heading to court. Complications in a case such as foreign assets, tax, trusts, business or commercial involvement, need to be considered, and you should receive advice as to whether a mediation is an appropriate venue for resolution of these complex matters.

Mediation is a voluntary process, so the key is that both parties must invest and be willing to cooperate for it to succeed. A large proportion of disputes taken to mediation are settled — as much as 85% if the internet is to be believed — so if you can get your former partner to the table, you have a good chance of settlement.

Arbitration

This forum is governed by the Arbitration Act, and like a mediation the parties participate in the selection of the arbitrator and timetabling of the hearing. However, unlike mediation, the arbitrator checks facts, finds fault, and makes a ruling. It is a more formal process than mediation, but not as formal as the courts.

The time and costs associated will likely be higher than mediation, and costs can be awarded against the losing side. Like litigation, the parties lose control of the process once an arbitration is instigated, and an arbitrator's decision is normally binding and enforceable by the courts.

Arbitration is most frequently used for commercial disputes, and advice and research indicate that this is a highly unusual method of dispute resolution for matrimonial, family, or relationship property cases. Many family lawyers do not suggest arbitration for family disputes because, should the outcome go against them, there is no right of appeal.

Litigation and 'going to court'

Litigation is a pathway which ultimately leads to a court case. Not many disputes make it all the way to the courtroom; the vast majority are settled before that happens. Along the way some of the other resolution processes outlined above may — or will — occur.

Litigation usually relies on having a lawyer to advise and represent you, whether in negotiations or in court. If you choose to go to the Family Court without a lawyer (and an increasing number of people are doing this for financial reasons), you will be presenting evidence and questioning other witnesses yourself. To do that you will need to be aware of the rules of the Court, and the relevant law. This information is available online through the Ministry of Justice, but be warned, you will need a lot of time available to come to grips with the law, the court requirements, and preparation of documentation.

Most people appoint a lawyer. Having done so, you will likely instruct them to attempt to negotiate with your former partner's lawyer. Before this negotiation can begin, evidence must be gathered so your lawyer has accurate information with which to make your case. This evidence may include valuations, financial analysis to determine the value of the assets to be divided, and further analysis of the law as it relates to your specific situation.

If the negotiation fails, a mediation may be proposed by either party. If everyone on both sides agrees that it is a worthwhile path to pursue, a mediation can be held using the information you have gathered. If the mediation is successful and results in a signed agreement between the parties, the matter ends here.

If, however, the mediation fails and further negotiation is fruitless, the options left to you are:

1. Do nothing.
2. File proceedings in court.

Doing nothing is a legitimate strategy and leaves the ball in your former partner's court, so it is up to them to review their position and either open negotiations again, or file in court.

Once proceedings have been filed, for a relationship property case, the process for 'court' is roughly to gather relevant information regarding property interests; to categorise property into relationship or separate property; then the court makes orders to divide the property on the basis of the Act, making whatever adjustments are allowable under the Act. This is, of course, a massive simplification of a rather complicated process!

While we start our relationships 'courting', some do end in court. The court process is expensive — often more than $100,000 from start to finish, and in general the cases which make it there have complicated issues and a large pool of assets. It is a process where a judge makes a ruling based on the facts of your case and your lawyer's advocacy skills. If either you or your former partner is not satisfied with the outcome of the court case, you can appeal to a higher court. If the higher court agrees to accept the case, you are back into round two, and more compliance costs and legal fees.

One positive aspect of proceedings is that it imposes a timeframe which must be adhered to, ensuring the case doesn't stagnate or is not prioritised. Simply filing in court doesn't mean you will definitely end up with your case being heard there. It is, however, regarded as a legitimate legal strategy which motivates both parties to settle, and if that doesn't happen, then the pathway to resolution in court is available without further delays.

Family Dispute Resolution

For separations involving children, the Ministry of Justice provides a Family Dispute Resolution mediation service which is aimed at reaching agreement without recourse to the court system, and within which parents or guardians are assisted to develop a sustainable and equitable parenting plan.

To access this service most people will need to attend a free course — Parenting Through Separation — conducted by experienced professionals and aimed at improving communication between all family members, focused on making decisions in the best interests of the children. Each parent usually attends different sessions to avoid conflict and disruption for the other people attending, and to ensure the parent attending can speak freely.

You may also need to attend pre-mediation, which is especially useful to help you manage if you are stressed or angry, and to help you focus clearly on your children's needs. The objective of the service is to resolve immediate parenting issues and to provide new skills to allow future issues to be resolved calmly.

In real life — just one path to resolution

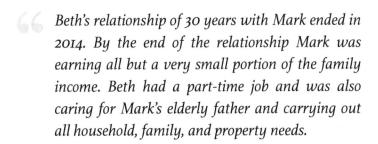

> *Beth's relationship of 30 years with Mark ended in 2014. By the end of the relationship Mark was earning all but a very small portion of the family income. Beth had a part-time job and was also caring for Mark's elderly father and carrying out all household, family, and property needs.*
>
> *Following separation, a brief attempt was made to divide joint property by direct negotiation, but Beth was out of her depth. 'Mark was a skilled negotiator, with close friends in the legal profession, and I felt I had no choice but to seek*

legal advice, so I appointed a senior lawyer to advise me,' says Beth.

Facts were noted, valuations prepared. A forensic accountant was appointed to analyse the facts and financials and determine the magnitude of any claim for economic disparity. The accountant also analysed Beth's entitlement to spousal maintenance and considered whether the business was relationship or separate property, and the implications for the family trust! A steep learning curve for Beth, but a legal strategy evolved from this initial process.

Beth's lawyer exchanged emails with Mark's lawyer. Beth notes, 'The time between emails was often slow — maybe a new valuation was required, or maybe the other side was waiting on an expert's report, or sometimes the lawyers were just tied up with other cases.' Three years and several thousand dollars into negotiations, Beth contacted Mark 'without prejudice' (meaning off the record) and asked him what asset split he 'really wanted to settle'. A figure was agreed, and Mark's lawyer documented it. When his draft agreement was received it contained further requirements which Beth's lawyer advised were totally unacceptable and so this attempt at settlement failed.

Beth was, by now, desperate but realised the urge to 'put it behind me' had to be tempered. She was *very aware that both she and Mark were experiencing grief, anxiety, change, and confusion, and each would arrive at a point where they could cope with the financial aspect at different times. 'My lawyer pointed out that a quick resolution can result in recriminations years later where one party feels they didn't understand all the issues at the time and may even believe their weakened emotional state put them at a serious disadvantage, but at that point there's nothing that can be done,' and so Beth waited.*

Following the failed attempt at direct negotiation, Beth was becoming more and more stressed and anxious. Her lawyer strongly advised Beth not to communicate with Mark. She suggested filing in court, but the cost and additional stress associated with that had no appeal, and so — after a pause of some months — negotiations continued, but again were fruitless.

In mid-2018, in frustration at the lack of progress, Mark decided to represent himself. Being fully aware of her financial limitations, Beth's lawyer suggested that she also represent herself and negotiate with Mark directly, checking in occasionally to ensure Beth didn't lapse into destructive or personal communication. Finally, an agreement was achieved and documented, and eventually settled just days before the fourth anniversary of the separation.

Beth clearly recalls the bittersweet moment late on a Friday afternoon when the email arrived with the news that the settlement was complete. 'I knew it was momentous, but it somehow didn't feel like a celebration, just an ending. It took a month or more for it to truly sink in that that part of my life was now actually over. While I had already "got on with my life" in many ways, knowing my financial situation meant I could make decisions about my future, without recourse to Mark.'

In real life —

Roger and his wife Anne took around three years to come to an agreement on the financial aspect of their separation. As Roger sees it, there were two significant areas to negotiate. The first was to agree the value of all their joint assets. The second was to agree the proportions of the division.

Anne had sacrificed her career to raise their children, but Roger had supported her to retrain when their children were young teenagers. He agreed the settlement should provide for a small degree of financial inequity.

Roger and Anne met regularly face to face to attempt to find a resolution. They didn't agree on either the valuation or the proportions initially, resulting in frequent exchanges of spreadsheets and disagreements as to values.

What ultimately helped Roger and Anne to reach agreement was to stop looking at the details set out in the spreadsheets and guessing at small changes in values, and to focus on the big picture — a 'global solution'. 'Just negotiating on the dollar value which would change hands was immensely helpful, and it was a huge relief to put it behind us,' says Roger.

While both Roger and Anne had access to legal advice, they were certain they could reach agreement with limited recourse to their lawyers other than to sign off the deal they made with each other.

NEW ZEALAND LAW

WHAT FOLLOWS IS a summary of the law as it relates to two key issues of separation and divorce — money and children. There is a wealth of detailed information on the New Zealand Law Society website (www.lawsociety.org.nz), however, you should consult your lawyer about how the law specifically applies to your situation.

Financial separation

In New Zealand, the rules for the division of property following the end of a relationship are set out in the Property (Relationships) Act 1976 (we will call this 'the Act'). Should your case make it to court, proceedings under the Act will most likely start at the Family Court but could be transferred to the High Court if they are sufficiently complex.

The Act provides the rules in New Zealand for the division of relationship property on separation or death of one of the parties. It has been significantly changed since 1976 to incorporate de facto relationships and civil unions.

A 'de facto relationship' is a relationship where both parties are 18 or over and have been living together as a couple for three years or more. There are further tests around what constitutes a de facto relationship, such as whether there is a sexual relationship and the sharing of funds, but we won't delve into these in detail here.

The only way to avoid the Act is to have a Contracting Out Agreement, referred to in detail later in this section, and in the section on new relationships.

THE ASSET POOL

Relationship assets, minus relationship liabilities, is referred to here as 'the asset pool'.

Relationship property

'Relationship property' consists of assets which are jointly owned. According to the summary provided by the New Zealand Law Society, this includes:

- The family home (unless it is on Maori land),
- Family chattels (furniture and fittings, household equipment and appliances, and vehicles, boats, etc.), even if they are registered to just one party,
- Other jointly owned property,
- In some circumstances, separate property which

has been intermingled with relationship property,
- Property acquired before the relationship began if it was intended for the couple's common use or benefit,
- All income earned and property bought after the relationship began, and
- The value added during the relationship to superannuation and life insurance policies.

Relationship property is valued at the date of a court hearing unless there are extenuating circumstances, or where negotiations are being carried out outside of court, by agreement between the parties. To avoid further disagreement, each party should have independent valuations.

Separate property

'Separate property' comprises assets that are owned individually. Again, using the New Zealand Law Society's information, this includes:

- Gifts,
- Inheritances (which have not been mingled with other property),
- Heirlooms and taonga,
- Property acquired under a trust,
- Property declared as separate in a Contracting Out Agreement, and
- Property acquired before the relationship began, and property acquired with the proceeds of

separate property and not intended for the use or benefit of both parties.

Debts

Personal debts are the responsibility of the person who incurred them, but joint debts are deducted from the total value of the assets. Joint debts include debts incurred for 'common enterprise' or family business, or for improving relationship property, or for the benefit of both parties in managing the household, and debts incurred bringing up children of the relationship.

Trusts

Trusts are common in New Zealand — as many as 50% of married couples have a trust, and these trusts must also be taken into account in separation negotiations.

Historically the purpose of a trust was to have property held by an outsider, effectively avoiding the rules set out in the Property (Relationships) Act 1976 because the property was not 'owned' by a party to the relationship.

There are, of course, many reasons to establish a trust, for example, estate planning, creditor protection, taxation, to provide for children from an earlier marriage, asset protection.

If a trust is established prior to commencement of a relationship and the only assets in the trust are those assets acquired prior to commencement, it is difficult to argue that those assets should be taken into account.

If, however, relationship property has been transferred or disposed of to a trust during the relationship, this can be taken into account in a separation if it had the effect of reducing the pool of relationship property. This is even more likely if it is believed that the purpose of the transfer to the trust was to deny a spouse their rightful share of relationship property.

While a court does not have the power to transfer the property back out of the trust, it can order compensation to be paid. This compensation will be by way of an adjustment of the share of relationship property from the other partner's separate property, or from trust income.

This is also true if, during the relationship, relationship property has been transferred into a company which is controlled by one partner in the relationship, and where the effect of the transfer is to remove the other partner's property rights.

Equal sharing

A key principle of the Act is that each party to the relationship is assumed to have contributed equally to the relationship and is entitled to an equal share in the relationship property. The intention is to give equal rights to a partner who has contributed more in non-financial ways to the relationship, such as caring for the family.

The Act has the ability to take the needs of children into account in any division of property, giving the court the power to award relationship property for the benefit of the children; or postpone division of property to prevent hardship to the principal carer of the children. It can make all sorts of orders to ensure the children have a home and are cared for.

Exceptions to the equal sharing rule

As mentioned, there are exceptions to the equal sharing rule. These are relationships of short duration; and where 'extraordinary circumstances' would make equal sharing 'repugnant to justice'.

A relationship of short duration is a marriage or civil union relationship of less than three years at the time of death of one of the parties, or at the time of separation. Under special circumstances it can also apply to a de facto relationship where the couple has a child, or if one party has made a substantial contribution to the relationship, but most importantly where it would be very unfair if property was divided equally. For legal purposes, the relationship starts when the parties start living together.

The test for the 'extraordinary circumstances' exception is hard to satisfy, but if the court determines that equal division would be totally unfair, the proportions of the asset pool to be divided will reflect the contribution of each party to the relationship.

Economic disparity

If, following separation, one partner will be significantly worse off than the other as a result of the effect of the 'division of functions' within the relationship, the disadvantaged partner may be awarded more than 50% of joint property, effectively redressing the economic disparity created during the relationship.

It's not enough for one partner to simply earn less; they need to show that this came about at least in part by the division of functions within the relationship. This is simply how the couple organised their lives — one partner may have supported the other during study, enabling that partner to advance their career; or one partner may have had greater or sole responsibility for care of children, forgoing their career advancement.

The likely earning capacity of each partner and their ongoing responsibilities for care of children will be taken into account when calculating economic disparity. A forensic accountant is frequently engaged to do this and prepare a formal report.

Payment of economic disparity is from relationship property, not from the other partner's future earnings (which is not relationship property), which results in an unequal division.

Contracting Out Agreements

The only way to not be bound by the Property (Relationships) Act is to enter into a Contracting Out Agreement under section 21 of the Act. This lets you set your own rules for ownership and division of property in the event that the relationship breaks down.

Contracting Out Agreements — or pre-nuptial agreements — are more common with second and subsequent relationships where the parties are more likely to have significant assets at the outset of the new relationship. They can be made at any time — even at the end of a relationship. A key component of a Contracting Out Agreement is to set out how future property is to be dealt with.

These agreements must be recorded in writing and signed off by each party's lawyer. The lawyer must certify that they have discussed the effect and implications of the agreement with you, with full disclosure and agreed values.

Ideally you should review these agreements every five to ten years to make sure they still reflect the wishes of both parties, particularly if there have been any major changes in the relationship or the law changes. You will be reminded of the importance of Contracting Out Agreements in the section discussing new relationships because they offer protection in the event of another relationship.

This all sounds complicated and difficult, but it is in your best interests. A court can set aside a Contracting Out Agreement *only* if it is very one-sided. If you have been properly advised, this is most unlikely.

Covering everyday living expenses — are you entitled to spousal maintenance?

In many relationships, one partner has a higher income than the other. For a 'reasonable' period of time after separation, the higher-earning partner has a responsibility to maintain the other partner, to the extent necessary to meet their reasonable needs. This is called 'maintenance', or 'spousal maintenance'.

This is likely to apply if the lower-earning partner has limited ability to self-support, or they care for children of the relationship. The standard of living of the parties while they were together is considered, as is any training being undertaken by the lower-earning partner with the objective of increasing their earning capacity.

A 'reasonable' period of time is very dependent on the particular situation — age, length of the relationship, and the lower-earning party's ability to become self-supporting — but could be up to five years. The amount of maintenance depends on the particular circumstances, particularly earning capacity and the needs of each party.

To determine this, your lawyer will ask you to prepare a budget showing what you expect your expenses to be while you are unable to pay your way.

In some circumstances a judge may decide maintenance payments are not appropriate, but this would require the lower-earning partner to have done something which is 'repugnant to justice'.

Children

The law relating to children is complex, but there is significant help available within the court system to ensure your family works successfully into the future.

Guardians

A guardian has legal rights to participate in all important decisions concerning the child's upbringing — from education to religion. In New Zealand the mother is the natural guardian of a child; but both parents are guardians of the child if they are in a relationship at any time beginning with conception to birth of the child.

There are support mechanisms available including a free programme called Parenting Through Separation which educates parents and guardians on communication with family members, aimed at providing the children of the relationship with the best possible outcome.

Living arrangements

If you decide to live separately from your partner, you both need to agree who the children will usually live with. Hopefully this can be done amicably, in the interest of the children, but if not, there are ways to resolve this.

The first would be to discuss options with a specialist counsellor, perhaps a relationship counsellor, or seek advice on how to handle this issue from a lawyer or Citizens Advice Bureau. If that is unsuccessful, you may have no alternative but to go to court to resolve the matter. Just remember at all times that the needs of the children are paramount, and it should be possible to find a workable solution which enables both parents be involved.

. . .

Abuse

If there is abuse — physical, sexual, psychological, financial — or harassment, there are mechanisms such as protection orders which are available to safeguard you or your child or children. The mechanics of how to handle abuse or harassment are not discussed further here, but your lawyer or the Family Court can advise and assist.

Financial assistance

Both parents have financial responsibility for the ongoing care of the children, and it's best if you and your former partner can work out an arrangement which suits you both. If that's not possible, the Child Support Agency is available to assist and make orders for payment of 'child support'. Generally, child support is paid until the child is eighteen.

The Inland Revenue Department has a formula which can be used to calculate payments, or you can reach agreement with your former partner. If that agreement fails for any reason, the IRD formula is applied. In both of these scenarios the IRD collects payments and pays them to the other parent. If you have a good relationship with your former partner, you can reach a private agreement and make payments without the need for administration by the IRD.

Remember, the children's needs are paramount. Manipulating custody arrangements to minimise payment obligations to the other spouse puts further stress on any future relationship with your children's other parent which could adversely affect your children.

Demystifying dissolution

The formal end of a marriage or civil union is called a 'dissolution' in New Zealand. Here, the only ground for legally dissolving a marriage or civil union is 'irreconcilable differences', and the only way to prove that is to live apart for two years.

Knowing your date of separation is very important but can be surprisingly difficult to ascertain. What if you just grow apart, and agree to not be in a relationship but continue living together? What if one of you takes a job overseas and you agree to travel between countries but at some point, the travelling stops? The time period of two years can't be shortened, for any reason, even if you both want it.

Either or both partners can apply for a dissolution, so long as at least one of you lives in New Zealand when the application is made.

There is no formal dissolution process for de facto relationships.

Legal lingo

A list of some of the legal terms you are likely to come across follows:

Adjournment — where a court hearing is postponed to another day.

Affidavit — a written statement which is sworn to be true by the person signing it. It is the same as any evidence on oath in court.

Appeal — a request to challenge and overturn a lower court's decision.

Arbitration — a form of alternative dispute resolution held before an arbitrator who will make orders.

Asset — something which is owned, for example, a building, property, or cash at the bank.

Assign — to transfer ownership of an asset to another person.

Barrister — a member of the legal bar who specialises in the court process.

Capital gain — the profit or gain when an asset is sold or disposed of.

Care of Children Act 2004 — the most recent piece of legislation covering the rights of minors in New Zealand and which places the minor as a paramount consideration.

Child — a person under 18 years of age.

Child Support Act 1991 — the law which regulates child support, managed by the Child Support unit of the Inland Revenue Department.

Child Support Maintenance — the amount of maintenance the parent not living with their child must pay.

Civil union — same-sex couples may enter into a civil union to create the same rights and obligations as a marriage.

Collaborative law or practice — a structured process in which parties to a dispute meet voluntarily with an impartial third party or parties to help them reach agreement.

Contracting Out Agreement — an agreement entered into between parties before a marriage often to regulate financial affairs should they separate or divorce.

Counsel — legal representation, frequently a barrister.

Custody — where the child resides and who with.

De facto relationship — for the purposes of the **Property (Relationships) Act**, a de facto relationship is a relationship between two people (whether of different sexes or the same sex) who are both aged over 18 years and are living together as a couple, but are not married to, or in a civil union with, each other. After three years of cohabitation, the relationship is protected by the Property (Relationships) Act.

Disbursement — a payment made to a professional person for services rendered, for example a barrister or accountant might charge an administration fee, photocopying, courier delivery charges in their invoice.

Dissolution order — the official documentation ending a marriage or civil union.

Expert witness — an expert in a particular field who is to provide a report, opinion, or evidence to a court.

Family Court — the Family Court is a division of the District Court and is where most family or relationship matters are heard.

Family Dispute Resolution service — a mediation service for families aimed at reaching agreement outside the court system.

Forensic accountant — a qualified accountant who specialises in examining data, frequently engaged to determine claims for economic disparity or to determine if any money is missing and how to recover it. They often act as expert witnesses in hearings.

Guardian — a person appointed to look after the interests of a child.

High Court — the highest court at which proceedings can be instigated.

Injunction — an order preventing a person from taking a specific step or action.

Judgment — a decision by a court.

Jurisdiction — where a court has the power to deal with a case and make certain orders.

Life assurance or insurance policy — a contract between the policy holder and the insurance company often to pay out in the event of death.

Litigation — the process of taking legal action before a court within proceedings.

Maintenance — child support, or money to be paid to the other partner.

Mediation — a process before an independent person (and not before a court) where parties attempt to reach an agreement and resolve a dispute.

Oath — swearing the truth of a statement.

Order — a direction, instruction, or command of the court.

Property (Relationships) Act — the law as it relates to the division of property following the end of a relationship.

Separation — when parties end a relationship, not necessarily limited to physical separation.

Solicitor — a lawyer who advises a party and provides legal advice.

Spousal Maintenance Order — an order that one party is to make periodical payments to the other for such term as may be specified by the order.

Statement of Financial Position — a statement setting out details of the parties' finances.

Trust — a financial arrangement under which a property or other asset is held by named people for another party.

Trust Deed — a legal document used, for example, to create a trust.

Trustee — a person who holds an asset on behalf of another party.

Undertaking — a formal and binding promise to the court which can be enforced.

Warranty — a term in a contract.

Will — a legal document where a person leaves money or other assets in the event of death.

Without Prejudice — a document which is marked as 'Without Prejudice' cannot be referred to within court proceedings and is commonly used when a person makes an offer.

Witness — a person who makes a statement and/or is to give evidence to a court.

LAWYERS AND LEGAL ADVICE

THERE IS a subtle difference between a solicitor and a barrister. Both have received the same fundamental training in the law, but a barrister generally specialises in litigation. You may engage a solicitor initially to try to negotiate a settlement, but if your case is filed in court, you may need a barrister to run your case. If so, your solicitor will advise on suitable barristers who have expertise in cases similar to yours. We will refer to solicitor and barrister interchangeably as 'lawyer'.

Do you need a lawyer?

If your relationship split is harmonious, you may well be able to resolve any issues by discussion and agreement. The agreement you reach will be in accordance with the Property (Relationships) Act and must still be signed and certified by a lawyer as set out in the resolution options section above.

If you need help with any area of the law — and let's face it, how many of us know the rules? — you need a lawyer. Hiring a lawyer is not 'required', and you are able to represent yourself but the cost of not fully knowing the extent and complexity of the law may be reflected in your financial settlement. Representing yourself also opens you up to focusing on issues which are important to you but are not strictly useful for your case.

However much you don't want to hire a lawyer, they are trained in the law and are required to follow standards of professional behaviour, including providing you with information about the service they offer. This includes how fees will be charged and when they are payable. The fee charged will depend on the lawyer's skill, specialisation, and experience.

Having engaged a lawyer to help you through your financial separation, unless there is a clear reason not to do so, take their advice! That's what you hired them for. From their past experience they will have a good idea of how your case will go — good or bad — so try to be realistic and open-minded about resolution options and compromise. It's worth repeating often that if you don't agree or don't understand what your lawyer is proposing, ask them to explain.

If you sign up with one lawyer but decide — for whatever reason — to change to another, you are absolutely free to do so. You will, of course, have to pay for work done to that point. If you are unhappy with a lawyer's behaviour you can raise this with the New Zealand Law Society.

Getting good value from your lawyer

There's no way around it, but whatever you spend on lawyers ultimately erodes the assets available for distribution, so whatever you can do to help your lawyer and save them time is in your best interests.

Some tips for getting good value from your lawyer:

- Being proactive and getting advice early on will stop you following an unproductive path.
- Don't sign anything important without having your lawyer read it first.
- Do some research yourself by reading up on the law using information available on the New Zealand Law Society website or the Citizens Advice Bureau website. This will at least mean you understand what your lawyer is talking about. Even just reading the legal chapter here puts you a step ahead of where you likely were before.
- Provide your lawyer with everything — don't hold back on some information because you think it will not benefit your case; this will inevitably be found out in the end, maybe to your detriment.
- Hold back from involving your lawyer in the emotional aspects of your case. This isn't law, and they are not counsellors.
- Present your information in a sensible and tidy way — documents in date order, maybe even

with an index to save your lawyer time. If you are well prepared, it will cost less.
- Think before you communicate, and only communicate on important matters. Every little 'what do you think?' email will cost you.
- Ask for quotes for all work and satisfy yourself that the work is necessary.

What if you can't afford a lawyer?

A limited amount of legal advice is available — free — from Community Law Centres or your local Citizens Advice Bureau. They, or your lawyer, will be able to advise you of your entitlement to legal aid, based on your circumstances. An increasing number of people fall into a financial crack between being eligible for legal aid and being able to afford a lawyer and are choosing to represent themselves in the Family Court.

Tell your lawyer your financial constraints and discuss ways to reduce cost. You may be able to negotiate a fee arrangement. You may also be able to help with research and other tasks to minimise costs.

Selecting the right lawyer

This is a difficult undertaking, with many options available. Ask around your friends and colleagues, phone a couple and gauge how you feel. You can also ask at a Community Law Centre or a Citizens Advice Bureau.

It's a personal decision and you will be sharing all your financial information and relationship issues with them, so it is important to find someone who you connect with, and who you trust. It's wise to interview your prospective lawyer and have them clarify or spell out anything you don't understand. Don't be embarrassed to do this — you are not expected to be an expert!

What follows is a short list of questions you could ask your lawyer before hiring them. Answers to some you will find on their websites, but others maybe not:

- Do you specialise in relationship property and family law?
- Do you have time to focus on my case?
- Do you have a strategy for my case? And how long should it take to resolve?
- If, at any point in the process, I want to negotiate with my partner directly, would you be amenable to that?
- How often will I be billed, and what is your hourly rate? Do you have other staff who will be working on my case, and if so, what is their hourly rate?
- Are there other costs I need to be aware of? For example, psychologists, accountants, private investigators; and how much do you expect those specialists to charge?
- How can I reduce costs? Is there anything I can do to progress the case myself?
- Do you have a guideline of the total financial cost

of this case? (The correct answer is probably that it is too difficult to estimate because there are so many ways in which the case can go, so if you are told an amount which appears reasonable, compare it to other answers you have received.)

THE COST OF SEPARATION

APART FROM THE significant personal cost in mental health and time, you will be faced with financial costs of various kinds. These could include legal fees, expert advice, court fees, not to mention the expense of counselling and coaching. Let's take a look at what these various costs might be.

Personal cost

The personal cost of a separation is immense, and a court case multiplies that. From a mental health perspective, it is a long, drawn-out process where your past is constantly present and the carrot of freedom tantalisingly just out of reach. You will feel positive one day and crushed another, and completely mentally drained most days! In the words of one experienced lawyer, 'The pain of separation does not begin until you actually separate.'

Expect to spend a significant amount of time responding to your lawyer and finding evidence of one form or another that they need for your case — from email records to finances, relevant dates, and all sorts of personal details. As a key participant in your case, only you can provide this information, and your active and prompt participation will be reflected in lower legal fees.

By its nature, the process of litigation exacerbates any suspicions you and your partner may have about the other, causing time and money to be spent verifying facts and strategising. The message here is that you need to be completely sure this can't be settled privately, out of court.

Lawyer's fees

There are ways to control legal costs and manage the legal process. Most important is to be well organised and thoroughly in touch with your case. Writing a clear outline for your lawyer of what the problem is and what you hope to achieve will help them but also help you to identify what you are wanting to achieve. Discuss this with your lawyer and agree on what is to be covered in their advice. Be very familiar with numbers and facts, check and recheck spreadsheets, calculations, and communications.

If you have a budget, share this with your lawyer and discuss before you start work. Keep track of fees as you work through your case and communicate any concerns to your lawyer. The costs of various forms of dispute resolution are vastly different and depend on many factors. There's nothing wrong with checking your invoices for accuracy. For example, if you notice the meeting you had with your lawyer was an hour long, but you are charged for two hours, ask them why. That extra hour may have been legitimately spent in preparing for the meeting or writing up notes from the meeting, but whatever it is, you want to know, and you are entitled to ask. Don't lose sight of the fact that it's your money being spent.

Your lawyer may have a junior lawyer working with them who will carry out research, prepare initial drafts of documents, and other work as required. The junior lawyer will charge at a lower rate, reflecting their experience, and can be a great first port of call for simple questions to keep costs down.

It's worth making the point that the amount you spend on legal fees isn't necessarily tied to the size of the asset pool, but rather the complexity of the case. So, if the pool of assets to be split between you and your former partner is small, the legal fees you will incur in reaching agreement as a percentage of the asset pool will be large. This seriously undermines what is available for both of your futures. If this is your situation, make the point to your former partner to see if it motivates them to settle.

Expert fees

Valuers, accountants, or psychologists will all charge, and their fees can be negotiated to some extent. As with your lawyer, be very clear about what the cost is before agreeing to use them and be sure you know what you are getting for your money.

Court fees

Should your case make it to court, there will be fees associated with this for filing documents. There is also the potential for the court to order you to pay costs, taking into account many factors. From past experience, your lawyer will be able to advise what these costs are likely to be.

All this sounds like a lot of money, and it is. Forewarned, however, is forearmed, so be assertive and ask if you think you have been overcharged; or speak up if you are spending more than you can afford.

PART 5
CREATING YOUR NEW (BEST) LIFE

While getting on with the hard stuff, it's easy to neglect yourself. There are many areas of your life which will have changed with the end of your relationship — not just finances and living arrangements, but, from a physical perspective, major stress has a big impact.

Taking care of your physical and mental self is essential both in the aftermath of the break-up and during any negotiations with your former partner. It's not unusual for people in high-stress situations to either gain or lose weight. When preparing meals for one, it's very easy to fall into habits of either not eating or binge eating. Similarly, alcohol or drug intake may change.

TAKING CARE OF YOURSELF

SO HOW DO you take responsibility for yourself? The importance of keeping yourself healthy cannot be stressed enough. If you are going through a difficult separation, you literally need to be fighting fit, which means a healthy diet and plenty of exercise.

Food

Pay attention to your diet from the simple perspective of nourishing yourself. If you are now living alone and finding it difficult to cook, there are ways to manage this. Apart from the good fresh food cook-at-home-but-don't-think delivery options available which make the cooking minimal, come up with a few meal ideas which are tasty and simple, and which can be prepared in bulk and frozen (good for the budget too). There's nothing quite as satisfying as reaching into the freezer and finding home cooking.

Being social

Food seems easier to prepare if there's someone to share it with, so how about inviting a friend or family member over? (Make sure there will be leftovers for the next night or two!)

While we are on this subject, friends can be a bit odd about socialising with a separated person and you may find yourself invited to a 'girls' night' or a rugby game or drinks with the boys, but not to dinner parties or outings with couples. Take the initiative and invite *both* people in a couple over or out for drinks to signal that you are not allergic to coupledom.

If you are invited out, unless you have an excellent reason not to do so, accept! Roughly 90% of the time you will feel better for it, believe me.

Exercise

Take care of your body with an achievable exercise regime. You may not feel up to an intense new workout plan, but your body needs to work to keep your brain on the level. Reaching out and joining an exercise class or group personal training session will help your motivation and has the additional benefit of bringing new people into your life.

It won't be news to you that exercise increases endorphins and other positive chemicals associated with feeling good.

Fitness also increases confidence, reduces anxiety and stress, and increases mental sharpness — just what you need!

Mental health

Your mental health is an integral aspect of your overall health. Allowing yourself to grieve will help you to move on. Not everyone around you knows how to handle what you are going through and you will find yourself the recipient of a lot of potentially unwanted or unsound advice and assistance!

Creating negative energy such as stalking your former partner on social media — or new people they may be forming relationships with — probably won't have the effect you want and can even have the opposite effect of furthering your resentment and increasing your pain.

Surrounding yourself with positive people and positive activities will help to keep you mentally on your game.

Feed your soul

This is an aspect of healing which is often neglected. There is comfort to be gained from other people's philosophical intuition whether it be in the form of phrases, musical lyrics, or lines from poetry. These can allow you to rise above your hurt, so if you find something which touches you and helps, make a note, and refer back to it when you need support.

There will be a time when you need catharsis, an opportunity to empty out your grief and anguish, or even anger and frustration. A good therapist or trusted friends can be enormously useful, just when you are ready. Dealing with these issues without support is much more difficult.

There are so many creative ways to feed your soul. Have a go at writing a haiku or find something beautiful to photograph — then do it every day for a month. Write a diary. Set yourself a goal of consciously doing one little thing for your soul every day. Whatever way you choose, be kind to yourself. If you want to watch Netflix all day every day while you work things out in your head, that's okay too — call it meditation.

Get help

Counselling is very useful when you are going through the emotional phase of your separation and is discussed in detail in the section on counselling above. It is an excellent way to sift through the events of the past and process feelings and reasons why you might be blocked from moving forward. Having worked through past relationship issues, you will be ready to move on to the next phase of your life.

Major life decisions shouldn't be made when there is turmoil, so having found a calm space, this is the perfect time to seek the advice of a coach. Coaches offer forward momentum by identifying issues, taking a close look at reality, and working with you to make a plan which fits the future you see for yourself. Discussing what you want from your new life with an independent professional allows you to explore more deeply and arrive at decisions which stick.

WHAT DO YOU WANT FROM YOUR NEW LIFE?

NO MATTER THE state of your old relationship or how you feel now it is over, it will leave a hole in your life. Filling that void can be a challenge, but it is also a rare opportunity for you to take stock and consider what you want out of the rest of your life. A scary thought, but immensely liberating — if you let it.

You may want a new direction in your work life but have not had the opportunity to take it. This could be that opportunity!

Outside of work there are new experiences to be had, new people to meet, and new hobbies to try. Many people in relationships have never had the chance to holiday alone or outside of their family group. 'Packaged tours' are a safe way to see the world and often don't work out to be any more expensive than sorting out your own itinerary and have the huge advantage of introducing you to a range of new people. You won't be alone — there are many people who book a trip for one. Your fellow travellers don't have to become your best friends, but they will be new and interesting.

Have you ever thought you'd like to contribute something to society and volunteer? There are hundreds of charities and organisations out there begging for help. Match your own interests to the charity to maximise the benefit to both you and the charity. Love horses? Align yourself with Riding for the Disabled. Love bikes? Find a charity which reconditions preloved bikes and gives them to kids. Love ...? You get the picture.

A group activity is always good for bonding with friends or colleagues. There are fun sports leagues, even for the non-sporty — go bowling! For the slightly sportier, how about something new like dragon boating or salsa dancing? It is daunting to enrol in teams or classes alone for the first time, but once you have done it once, it will get easier and easier.

As you open yourself up to trying new things, new people will emerge and new friendships form. Take your time; everything is a challenge initially and baby steps are the best way forward. As you become more confident you will be surprised at the opportunities which present themselves.

In real life — a road to recovery

 After my relationship ended, I lost interest in some activities which had been huge in my life to that

point. I no longer wanted to read. Cooking was a chore. I spent three months working my way through Netflix and just getting by on my own, learning to be alone. It was an odd and lonely time, not sure who I could share how I felt with, and not even sure who my friends were. I was a strange mix of euphoric and depressed, not sure what to do with myself in any area of my life. I had lost not only my relationship but my job as well.

Having got to the end of Netflix (only partly joking there), I slowly became able to face the massive task of sifting through the family belongings to make the home feel like mine. It became something of a macabre hobby, one cupboard at a time, making an enormous pile for my former partner to collect. The result was that I unwittingly created the 'head space' to actually begin to move on.

When I felt ready, I started dating online — another 'hobby' which can fill as much time as you let it. It was good for me to meet new people, go to new places, and most importantly not fall into another relationship straight away! I knew I needed some real time alone before I would be ready for that. Acknowledging that fact was liberating.

I had always wanted to go to India, so I booked a group tour and just went, ignoring protests from my parents. It was an amazingly positive learning experience for me. Building on my new-found confidence, I took myself to the other side of the world to visit my daughter who had been living there since before I separated from her father. It was a necessary — and occasionally difficult — trip as we tussled with the new format of the family, but immensely rewarding and an absolute joy to have had the opportunity to spend time with her, alone, on her turf and on her terms.

Over the next few years, I developed a new career which I love. I enter walking events in interesting places with friends. I re-engaged my love of cooking. I travelled alone to Japan to visit my son. I took up swimming for fitness and swam naked in Sydney Harbour in a group charity event. I have had fun rediscovering the joy of (bad) childhood table tennis. I hike and stay in DOC huts. I value my relationship with my adult children and devote time to them. I fired the chap who had been mowing my lawns for 20+ years and bought my own mower. I bought an e-bike and plan to try cycle touring. With each new experience, another world opens up. I have no idea what will come next but am keen to find out!

There's nothing amazing or particularly original about my journey, but I do recommend just incrementally giving new things a go, finding new people, having new experiences.

TAKING CONTROL OF YOUR FINANCIAL LIFE

A HUGE STRESSOR post-separation is not knowing your financial position. You can have a reasonable guess given the relationship assets and liabilities, but you may be facing legal fees and other unanticipated expenses which will erode your share of the asset pool.

Until you are financially settled with your former partner you will likely feel in some sort of limbo, but that's no reason not to start taking control of what you can and getting on top of your present and future needs. The way to start is to develop a budget.

Where will you live?

Many unhappy relationships continue because the financial cost of dividing the property is just too high. With escalating house prices — and the cost of renting always on the rise — this is hardly surprising.

Most couples will be forced to sell the house to enable the assets to be divided. This can be traumatic not just emotionally but may also leave you without enough cash to purchase separate properties or pay for rental on two properties. Taking the time to calmly consider how this can be handled will take some of the stress out of the situation later.

Is your pool of relationship property large enough to afford two dwellings? If not, the additional costs of renting or borrowing will need to be taken into account.

Budgets

Who managed the finances in your relationship? If it was you, you probably know about budgeting. Even so, don't skip this section — have a quick read to remind yourself of what you now need to do for yourself. If your former partner was in charge, this is your chance to upskill.

Knowing what your income and outgoings are enables you to plan ahead and gain control. Your budget can — and will — change over time as your needs change. Your immediate needs post-separation will be quite different to how you see your financial future, say, five years from now.

For a budget to be useful, it must be accurate. There's no point making a budget but leaving out what you spend on counselling because you think you might not need that in the future, or the cleaner because you plan to start doing the cleaning yourself. They are legitimate expenses and should be accounted for.

The budget you are creating needs to be realistic and workable. If you create a budget which is impossibly hard to stick to, you won't stick to it. Everyone needs to spend some money on 'feel good' purchases, and allowance for these sanity-savers must be factored in.

If you are entitled to spousal maintenance, your lawyer will ask you to create a budget which demonstrates what funds you need to maintain a reasonable standard of living while you are getting yourself back on your feet. This could even mean the time you need to retrain. The shortfall between income and expenses is what you might be entitled to.

To start creating your budget, record what you spend and earn. Using a spreadsheet is the easiest way to do this, but if that's not in your skillset, a piece of paper and a calculator will do the trick. There are example budgets online, free, such as at www.sorted.org.nz, which also has a budgeting tool.

Outgoings

Most transactions are electronic, which makes analysing your finances much easier because almost all of your expenses and income will be recorded in your bank statements.

Using the last three months of bank statements and invoices, make a list of your expenses and categorise them into columns. These could be house maintenance, power, rates, personal expenses, food, etc. Don't forget any cash you have withdrawn and what you spent it on. Some expenses are seasonal, like power, which could increase dramatically in the winter months, and this will need to be factored into your budget.

Make a separate list of expenses that are not covered in that three-month period which you pay annually or irregularly such as insurance, medical expenses, or gifts. Discretionary spending also needs to be taken into account such as holidays or clothing.

Income

This is money you receive from a job, superannuation, income from investments, as well as any government assistance in the form of benefits or allowances. Remember any cash you receive.

Creating your budget

From this information you can create your future budget. Assess your expenses and closely consider whether they are excessive or punitive. Ask yourself what you can *realistically* change: maybe a review of your entertainment expenses — can you ask friends over for a drink rather than going out? Maybe take a look at your wardrobe and revive some old favourites. Do you have time to develop an interest in your garden? Buying a lawnmower and hedge trimmer might be a small investment which will save you many hundreds of dollars over the coming years, with the side benefit of personal satisfaction!

Thinking about each expense item from your analysis, note at the foot of each column the amount you think is realistic for that expense item. Incomes are usually less flexible than expenses, so unless you plan to change your income by changing your work hours, for example, your income figures can be incorporated into your budget as they stand.

These new figures are your budget. If you have a shortfall, don't panic or throw away your budget! Take a deep breath and consider your options. There are always options.

Surplus or shortfall?

If the amount of income is greater than your expenses, you have a surplus. If expenses are greater than income, you have a deficit, or shortfall.

You have already trimmed your expenses in the process of creating your budget — do you still think they are realistic? If not, make some adjustments. Once you are happy with your expenses, consider how you can increase your income to manage any shortfall:

- Are you entitled to or are you receiving assistance from your former partner?
- Are you entitled to any government support? For example, you may qualify for a benefit if you find yourself unable to find suitable employment and you don't have savings to support yourself.
There's no shame in asking for help if you need it.

- Can you increase your income from employment?
- Do you have a spare room which could be rented out?
- Think outside what you have done before — is there anything else you can do to increase your income?

While not 'income', you may have assets you can sell. Obviously if you have yet to settle financially with your former partner, relationship assets are not able to be put up for sale, but you may have personal 'separate assets' which you no longer need, and the money put to work on your future.

A lot of pressure to spend comes not only from our own expectations and history, but also from peer pressure. If your friends are used to you having a certain level of income allowing you to participate in expensive activities such as a trip away, it may be a good idea to bring them up to speed on your new circumstances. If you don't, you risk overspending and even putting yourself in debt to keep up. No one is saying you shouldn't participate in social activities, but it may be a more significant part of your budgeted discretionary spending than it was before, so just consider your priorities.

If you still can't make ends meet, a further revision of more significant areas of your life may be needed. These could include downsizing or moving to less expensive accommodation; even changing where you do your grocery shopping can make quite a difference to your monthly food bill. Consider each expense item carefully and make enquiries of your providers as to how you can reduce your bills — mobile phone plan, electricity provider, health insurance plan, for example.

Financial advisers

If your budget resulted in a surplus, lucky you! A surplus is a nice problem to have, but you may need financial or investment advice to develop a plan for what to do with it. Also, if your settlement results in investments or cash on your side of the ledger, it would be wise to seek advice on how to manage this.

In the time before a financial settlement is reached, the financial focus needs to be on just getting through and making ends meet. This can be difficult with limited resources, particularly when your expenses are likely to have increased with legal fees, maybe even with the costs of setting up a new home. Knowing the asset base — your future — is being wound down every day is very challenging.

After settlement, life begins afresh, not least financially. This is your opportunity to really sort your finances and a great way to start is to engage a financial adviser to talk you through basic financial planning. Essentially, what do you need?

A financial adviser will outline the building blocks which are necessary for a secure financial future while looking out for yourself. These building blocks are cash management, insurance, and planning.

Cash management

This is simply making ends meet using the budgeting advice in this section, always ensuring the needs of your children are met. Depending on your stage of life, this is the time to really think of what *you* need.

Living insurance

It's important to have sufficient insurance to clear any debt, should things go badly wrong with your health. If you can afford it, insurance to cover bills if you are unable to work, or to clear debt should you become gravely ill is worthwhile, as is income protection insurance.

Retaining your hard-won financial independence, especially in the event of a new relationship, is the objective now. You don't want to go through all that again! With this in mind, consider carefully how your insurances are owned, for example, using a trust. This could become relevant in a new relationship where your insurances could become relationship property with your new partner.

Many people, including your lawyer, may advise you to cancel everything, but this can lead to a worse outcome in the future — especially in the case of medical insurance. Insurance contracts can be easily separated into individual parties — insurers know that separation is quite common!

A financial adviser will tell you medical insurance should never be cancelled if you are over thirty. This is because the medical insurer will assess your health and consider 'pre-existing conditions'. These could be any issue they identify — maybe something you have claimed for already which recurs, or anything they determine you are likely to get in the future, and it could cost you in increased premiums, or — worse — being declined insurance. To reduce your premiums, consider a less comprehensive plan or elect to pay an excess.

While we are on the subject, make sure your health and other insurance are in your personal name, not your former partner's — your medical records should be private. If you have young children, their insurance should be attached to the insurance of the person who takes them to the doctor and should be paid for by the main income earner.

Plan

Thinking ahead to when you are not working any more: where is your income going to come from? This is a terrifying thought for the person in the relationship who wasn't the main income earner, but it's best to plan carefully for this now.

Also discussed above in budgeting, a fine example of not thinking ahead is the need for retail therapy when your relationship breaks up — we have all done it. A new pair of shoes won't affect your financial future too much, but a new car might. This is not gender-specific!

Without wishing to make this worse than it already is, whatever you spend now comes out of your retirement funds, but with careful planning you can make the adjustments necessary now to live well, long after your work life has ended.

Wills and enduring powers of attorney

An essential part of planning is changing your will. This is addressed further below but is worth a mention here also. When you get married or enter a civil union, your old will is automatically revoked. This is not the case when your marriage ends. Your old will remains in force until you make a new one. This is the same for any enduring powers of attorney you hold.

Many people get stuck on deciding the details of their will. Who will be the guardians of the children? Who will be your executors? But if you treat your will as a living document, you can change it as often as you wish. It doesn't need to cost money; there are plenty of simple options available online, free.

If you do want legal advice on how to set up your affairs as you move forward in your life, think about using a lawyer who is not the one dealing with your break-up.

In the words of one particular financial adviser, 'Everyone has an opinion, so be careful and seek a qualified one.' Whatever your financial situation, understanding where you stand and gaining control is the key to moving forward.

TAKING CONTROL OF YOUR WORK LIFE

THIS SECTION ASSUMES YOU NEED — or want — to find new employment. Many people find themselves un- or under-employed when their relationship ends. There could be many reasons for this — perhaps one party to the relationship was more involved in raising the family or spent more time on unpaid tasks and were not in a position to develop their career.

If you have a job that you are generally happy with, hang on to it. Some stability is important when all else is in turmoil.

If you have not worked for some time, or worked part-time, this can result in a loss of confidence, not to mention a hole in your CV. You may see other issues as roadblocks which prevent you from moving forward with employment — maybe a lack of technical savvy, your age, or an inability to find work in the area in which you are familiar. These factors can be addressed. Sound like you? Read on.

Don't despair, you are never too old to try something new, and there are many options available to you.

New horizons

It could be that you are not sure what you want to do, in which case this is a rare opportunity to find out. Ask yourself some questions about what it is that you want — maybe even think back to what you were interested in when you left school, or at some time in your younger life.

A career coach or life coach can work with you to help sort out a direction which matches your aspirations and how to achieve them. These professional advisers have resources you may not have thought of and will challenge you with provocative questions to find out what's important to you and what your key skills are, and help you match those to employment options.

It's not cheap, but, like a CV writing service, is an investment which can pay dividends in the long run. When you reach a decision about a direction, consider any retraining you may need. There are many more options available than there were when we first trained, both in person and online. Think outside the box — maybe an apprenticeship!

While you are considering your options, there's 'temp' work which you may be qualified or even over-qualified for. This can be a way to get out in the world, back in the workforce, at a level you are comfortable with, especially if confidence has taken a beating from having been out of the paid workforce.

Don't dismiss the idea of starting your own business — little beginnings as a contractor, sole trader, or mini business start-up can grow into a self-made job. If you have an idea or a skillset you think you may be able to market or develop, check out the competition by going online. If it still stacks up, draft a plan for the business, talk to anybody who can help, seek any training you may need (not neglecting basic business skills), and start marketing yourself.

In real life — so what do you want?

> When trying to settle on an occupation which fitted her future, Sarah organised a chat with a close friend who was training to be a life coach. 'I was her guinea pig.' The coach started with a 'values exercise' asking questions about what was important to Sarah in any future job or occupation she chose. 'That's what was important to ME, not to my ex-partner or children,' says Sarah.
>
> After considerable discussion, Sarah worked out how she wanted to work, but not what she actually wanted to do. The next part of the process was to spend time thinking about her skillset and what could fit her values. Sarah frequently

referred back to her friend who was able to offer sensible commentary and would ask questions about each of her ideas. 'It was fantastic to feel I wasn't doing this alone, but that she was "along for the ride", open to talking through anything as it came up.'

Sarah's personal values included flexibility, work from home or work from anywhere, she didn't mind if she didn't have colleagues (being used to that in her previous work life), and she wanted just enough money to 'pay my bills and live independently. I wasn't trying to save for an elaborate retirement because I knew, in my fifties, I just didn't have time for that.' With the thought that she was likely to need to work past the normal age of retirement, what she settled on needed to fit that criterion, at least at some level.

Sarah's friend coached her through developing a business plan for what turned out to be a false start, but which fitted the values decisions she had made. 'It was really helpful to have a person with no stake in my future encouraging me to keep making plans and keep the forward momentum going. In a strange way I felt accountable to her, as if she was almost a part of my business.'

Sarah eventually settled on a different micro business model, working for herself. That business has mutated into what she happily does now, 'any day or time, to suit myself'.

Marketing yourself

It's a busy market out there and you are aiming to stand out from the other applicants and get an interview. Pull favours, ask friends and relations, make contact with old colleagues if you think they may be able to help you. Unfortunately, most of us have experienced 'it's not what you know but who you know' — don't fight it, get amongst it!

The first absolute must task when marketing yourself is to assess what sort of state your CV is in. A CV is your key personal marketing tool and should be a positive reflection of your *relevant* work history. If yours is seriously out of date or you have never had one, this is when you sort that out. There are plenty of examples of CVs available online, and advice about what to include.

If you don't know where to start, and preparing your CV is too much of a challenge for you, consider using a CV writing service. They will create a professional-looking CV which promotes your skillset and can focus your CV on a particular sector or position.

Even if you haven't worked for some years, you still have skills which can be promoted in your CV. Did you organise family holidays, help with homework, cook all the family meals while vacuuming? You are organised, flexible, and can multitask. These are valuable transferrable skills which an experienced CV writer will work into your CV, aligning your skills with the position you seek. These services don't necessarily require a huge cash outlay but are an investment which can pay dividends when your professional CV gets you an interview.

Along with your CV you will need a cover letter. This is more specifically tailored to the job you are applying for and should be adjusted for *every* application. It's best to send five well-crafted job applications for jobs you are actually interested in than broadcasting your CV to 20 potential employers. A generic CV and cover letter is easy to identify and will be quickly overlooked when the recruiter has hundreds to assess. According to Google, you have around seven seconds to get their attention; it has to be enough to take you to the next step. Again, a CV writing service will help with drafting a cover letter.

Apart from using your contacts, phone around recruitment agents to find out who specialises in the area you're interested in, arrange an appointment, and take your CV along. Don't be shy.

Ready to give up? Please don't!

You may already be familiar with rejection from other areas in your life, and you are likely to experience rejection here also. This is not a reason to give up.

For every job there are likely many applicants and only one can succeed. The successful applicant is often the one who is already known to the business prior to the position being advertised or is promoted by an agent working with the business. This doesn't mean you shouldn't bother looking on Seek or Trade Me Jobs; just be prepared for the competition. Rejection is a part of the process and you need to be tough and not take it personally.

Believe in yourself and your skills; don't be afraid to ask the recruiter why you didn't get that particular job — you can learn from the experience and adjust your approach for the next position that comes up.

Prejudice does exist in the employment market, and usually the person exhibiting prejudice or bias isn't even aware they are doing it. Employers are under a legal obligation to behave in an unbiased way regarding race, religion, sex, and age, however, the reality is that unconscious bias creeps into the decision-making process. Do what you can to minimise the opportunity for bias in your application; a CV writing service can also help here.

In real life — making work

> When I separated in 2017, I had skills, but not a lot of formal workplace experience. My former partner agreed to pay spousal maintenance, giving me time to regroup.
>
> Over the course of the next year, I applied for a number of jobs but didn't get even one interview. Looking back on this time, I can see this was probably a reflection of the state my head was in rather than the job market. I assumed, however, that at 56 years old I was now on the employment scrap heap, and I half-heartedly attempted to start

a business. While musing over my occupation dilemma I started writing; it made me feel I was doing something. By November 2018 I had completed a novel (a trashy one) and put it in a drawer.

Sitting at my desk in January 2019, 16 months after separation, tweaking a website I had organised for the half-hearted business, an advertisement for a course in proofreading and copyediting flitted over my screen. Thank you, Google, how did you know? I was really excited at the idea — it offered a chance to build on an aspect of my skillset which I had utilised in a small way in previous employment. I felt confident I could do it, and do it well.

I started the 12-month online course and completed it in six months. During that six months I converted the website into one marketing my new proofreading and editing business and started making contact with friends and former colleagues. In time, the business grew and evolved. By the end of 2019, I had proofread my novel, twice, submitted it and been accepted for publication.

In January 2020, during a lull in the academic year, I trained for a contract position writing CVs, so I added that new skill to my proofreading and editing business.

Friends and others I have talked to about my journey through separation and coming out the other side — including dating — have told me I should market myself as a dating coach. Now I occasionally write dating profiles and help others work through the online dating process.

And on it went — the students I worked with wanted CVs; the lawyer I used during my separation recognised my affinity with words and sent me a job advertisement for a contract position as a writer and copy editor, which I got; one of my master's level proofreading students put me forward for a contract writing position at her workplace, which I also got.

So, in a roundabout way, now I'm a writer!

TAKING CONTROL OF YOUR LOVE LIFE

OFTEN, not long after you have separated (and sometimes long before you are ready to forge a new life), you will be asked (frequently) when you are going to 'get back on the horse'. Literally, in those words. If you have been in a relationship for more than 10 years, dating has really changed. The time between ending a relationship and starting dating is very individual and you may find yourself encouraged out when you are just not ready. However, life can be lonely without someone to share it with, and most people find themselves seeking company eventually.

A lot will depend on whether you were the person who left or who was left. If you left, this may be an experience you were looking forward to, and you may even approach dating with what appears to be unseemly haste. If you are the person who was left, it may take a little longer for you to get to that point, but you will get there. There are no hard and fast rules.

While many men will already be back on the horse, women will often respond with a definite no thanks, and a reason why: *I've shut up shop — for ever! ... No thanks, I've had enough of men and relationships ... At my age? I'm never taking my clothes off in front of anyone again ... I can't be bothered with all that getting to know someone — it will just end badly anyway ... Why would I open myself up to more rejection?*

Sound familiar? Fair enough, maybe you're not quite ready. Everybody reading this book has had bad experiences in past relationships, but time changes the effect of these negative experiences, and one day you might feel the urge! Let's hope so. Having said that, many people are happy alone, satisfying their social needs in other ways.

Successful relationships can start at different life stages. You could meet at 50 and still have a very happy 30+ years together — it happens.

Short or long relationships can be equally devastating, emotionally and financially, when they end. The recovery process is frequently long, regardless of your role in ending the relationship. People often believe they are 'fine', but common wisdom shows it takes three to five years to fully recover. This is good to know — don't rush anything, and, as you will read elsewhere in this book, don't expect too much from yourself in the early months.

Dating

You are, of course, free to make your own choices, but let's just address what would happen if you *did* decide to 'get back on the horse'.

If you have been in a long relationship, the prospect of entering the dating world can be daunting. Traditionally people relied on luck to find someone, and you may be lucky enough to connect with a friend of friends at a dinner party or on a blind date, or an old flame may turn out to be just what you wanted all along; you may be a member of a club, church, or sports team which gives you access to unattached people. However, while younger people might find someone at university or work, through school friends or parties, it is an unfortunate reality that finding a new relationship in these more organic ways is more difficult.

Welcome to online dating! Home of over 40% of all new relationships. Despite the wise counsel of your friends who are in long relationships or your parents who rubbed along together for 50+ years, it's not all bad. And believe it or not, the stigma which once surrounded online dating is significantly reduced — just ask your kids.

Before the internet, the difficulty was availability — you just didn't meet many eligible singles! Compatibility was, as a consequence, a lower priority, which may explain why you are reading this book now. Dating apps and websites mean the availability of potential partners is high, so the focus of dating in this way is entirely compatibility.

Yes, dating is complicated, and you most likely won't find your perfect match on your first date (or your second or third). It is also interesting, and it gets you out of the house and meeting new people.

Enough of the preamble, let's do it.

Before we begin

Actually, let's not. We need to work out first whether you are ready to take the plunge, and what it is you hope to get out of dating. And you need to know how to keep yourself safe.

Are you ready?

Humans quickly form routines, and the routine of being alone is just one. So, are you ready to try something new? If you are working through a difficult financial separation with a difficult partner while juggling kids and work, it's understandable you may want to get through that before launching yourself into a new relationship. It's less understandable to restrict yourself socially, and dating can be simply that — meeting new people, extending your circle, going to new places and having some fun.

Have you worked out what it is that's holding you back? Most frequently it is fear of the unknown. It takes courage to step out of your comfort zone — but, remember, you have already done that simply by not being in your old relationship.

A common theme amongst men and women who are holding back from dating is poor body image. In conversation on this issue, many women state categorically they would never take their clothes off in front of another man. Some are conscious of their bodies even in front of their husbands. Men are not immune to poor body image either and, while they may not be so vocal about it, they are also acutely aware they are not quite as they once were. As we age, we look back on our lovely young selves, but the truth is that we are more interesting, more comfortable socially, and frankly more fun as we get older.

When 'promoting' yourself online, via your profile and photos, be honest. You'd be surprised at the number of women who write that they are more into 'dad bods' than gym junkies, and the number of men who are looking at profile photos to gauge personality through a smile, not waist measurement or bra size.

What are you looking for?

There are many reasons to start dating, none of them wrong, but it's good to know what your reasons are before you start. It helps when you are writing your profile if you can say you are looking for companionship and walks on the beach with the dog, or a relationship, or new sexual experiences. (If you are looking for new sexual experiences, perhaps be a little more euphemistic than that!) Your objectives can change over time, and you can change your profile or dating platform to suit.

When you are ready for a new relationship, different factors will be more important. As you meet new people on this journey, it's a good idea to develop some 'non-negotiables'. Depending on your personal situation, one of these could be economic compatibility. Unless you are seeking a sugar daddy (or mummy), if the person you are dating has significantly more assets or disposable income than you, it can place a financial burden on you to keep up and can even create a dependence on the person you are dating. If you are the person with the higher asset base, you are at risk of gaining a dependant!

There are many other more personal factors such as physical characteristics, personality traits, sense of humour, or even the type of activities they enjoy. Just be aware of your preferences and needs and stick to your non-negotiables.

Keeping yourself safe

One reason for not dating online is that it is widely considered to be dangerous. Following some simple rules will help to mitigate any danger. This is a concern particularly for women.

On your first date, never let your date pick you up from your home. You may think you know him or her from chats you have had, but there's nothing like meeting face to face to get the true measure of a person. Have someone drop you off, take public transport, or get a taxi.

The second rule is to always meet in a public place — either out in the open, perhaps a walk where there are other people around, or in a café, bar, or restaurant. A coffee date is a great way to see if there is compatibility and is easy to cut short if there's no connection.

Third, tell someone that you are going on a date. If possible, tell them where you are going and when you expect to be back, then update them when you get home or if you change your plans. I know this sounds unreasonable and possibly embarrassing, but it's a worthwhile precaution. A friend of mine tells her 80+ dad when she's heading out on a date!

Finally, a drink before your date to steady the nerves is not a good idea. If you are a bit nervous already, the next drink could cause poor decisions.

It's usual after a brief message exchange on an app to move off the dating platform and message privately. This is generally because the dating platform messaging system is clunky and is actually a good idea. If you meet straight off a platform like Tinder, you don't even know your date's phone number and, once a Tinder profile is deleted, it's impossible to locate the person or review your chat messages should something go wrong when you meet. It's best to have exchanged actual text messages or phone calls before you go on a date.

This is all just precautionary, good advice — forewarned is forearmed. Use your judgment but keep an eye out for odd behaviour.

But how do I do it?

Your dating profile

What should you put in your profile? Be honest, be funny, and be brief. Everyone has a past, and there's no need to be specific about what that is — it's a point of commonality which you can chat about on a date. Briefly describe your key attributes and what you are looking for in a match.

You need more than one photo, and all your photos should be fairly recent, with at least one full length. Try not to have too many selfies and not too many group pictures — the person looking wants to match with *you*, not your friends and family; and include photos of you doing things you enjoy. For example, if you're into horse riding, include a photo of that. If you don't have appropriate pictures, take some!

It's simple. Don't overthink it and remember you can change it as your objectives change. If you are not connecting with people you are interested in, don't give up, just change your profile or switch to a different dating platform!

If you find yourself struggling with what to include, and this has become a reason not to go online, ask for help. There are dating coaches who will chat to you about your objectives and help to put together your profile. It doesn't need to cost a lot and (like a great CV) is a small investment in your future.

The primary rule, as with any marketing, is think about your audience. If you want to attract a woman who likes motorbikes, include pictures of your bike. If you want to attract a man who likes to travel, include travel pictures.

Selecting and swiping

Once you have selected the dating app you are comfortable with and created your profile, you can start looking at prospective matches. It can be quite intimidating, especially if you are presented with a lot of potential matches and have no idea how to choose.

It is worth noting here that — at least on Tinder — if there is no location shown, it means the person is a paid subscriber and has elected *not* to show their location. This could be innocent — maybe they are travelling to wherever you are and want to make some connections beforehand — or it could be that they are wanting to hide their location for some reason, possibly not a good reason. Once you start chatting, there are scam indicators to look out for which are described later, but the rule of thumb is that if it looks too good to be true, it probably is.

Now *some* men will swipe on anyone, without really looking or reading. They then make their decision *after* a match has been made, which explains why they don't always reply! It's frustrating behaviour and there's no way around it, so move on to the next if this happens to you. It's not personal. Women generally closely read profiles and inspect photos, making careful decisions before swiping, creating a huge mismatch in behaviour. Some platforms, like Bumble, only allow women to make the first contact, which goes some way towards mitigating this problem.

How you make your selection is entirely personal, but profiles with more than one photo and at least some bio information shows thought and effort has been put into the profile.

That's really all there is to it — you get a glimpse into each potential match's world, what they look like, what they have to say about themselves and what they are looking for. It's brief, but a good indication.

Matching and meeting

So, you are all set up online and *ping*, you have a match! Well, don't leave them hanging, say hello! Many women will leave it to the man to start a conversation, but that's not necessary. Believe it or not, relationships are more likely to succeed if the woman starts the conversation.

It's normal to feel apprehensive, but because your photos and profile are an honest representation of who you are, there's really nothing to fear — just start chatting. If you find yourself really interested in your match, let them know. A meeting fairly early on bypasses the conversation becoming stale, and lets you move on if they are really not your type. Besides, you will have ticked off meeting a new person!

The first first date will be strange. There's no way around it. You will find — somewhat surprisingly — that you have things in common. Dating online is one of them, and often initial conversations include some discussion of dating experiences, and how you ended up on the app. You already know something of your date's life from their profile and your message conversation, so have a quick refresh before leaving to meet them.

Whatever happens, nothing rides on it and this is all valuable experience. You either like the person or you don't; if it's hard work or conversation doesn't flow, you're talking to the wrong person. It's nobody's fault, just a mismatch. Let your date know with a message afterwards how it was for you.

Troublemakers and scammers

There's no denying they are out there, and there's no truly reliable way to identify them in advance, but there are some warning signs to look out for:

- They quickly provide a lot of detail about their lives, and are generally foreign but living in the US, for example. The foreign aspect is intended to explain odd language structure.
- They are hard — or even impossible — to pin down to a date or time to meet.
- They communicate at odd times, not strictly in accordance with the time zone they are meant to be in.
- They won't do a video call.
- They mirror yourself back at you.

They are skilled manipulators who quickly work out what you are looking for and provide it, with a twist.

In real life — handsome, slim, tanned, foreign, fake

> 'I feel so foolish telling this story, but since this experience I have met many other people who have fallen into the same or similar scenarios,' says Meredith.

She recounts: 'He was pretty cute on paper — handsome, slim and tanned, American with German heritage. His profile had just the one picture — suited and professional; his location was hidden, and he was looking for love. He asked how long I had been on Tinder (one day) and of course he had also been on only three days. Almost immediately after we started chatting, he asked to move off the Tinder app and he was attentive and empathetic, fascinated by my relationship woes and petty dramas. The knight to my damsel.

'He asked for my email address because he was going to be travelling, and within a week or two he was sending me long love letters. He was planning on moving to New Zealand to retire but, before he came to visit me, he had to go to eastern Europe for a very lucrative business trip. The detail was extraordinary and totally believable. While he was there, he found he no longer had access to his funds — he even sent me his login details so I could let him know exactly how much was in his account and transfer a small amount to him. Of course, it was more than US$1m. The bank

> *transactions I did for him from his own account didn't work, and eventually he asked if I could lend him money to get a flight back because, as well as his access to cash issues, his project had run into problems.*
>
> *'I said no, I wouldn't pay for anything since we hadn't met. He was insistent. I was his only hope. Finally, he was angry and just stopped all communication.'* Meredith was 80% taken in up to the point when the love letters started arriving, but was curious so continued the ruse to see what would happen next. She was lucky. It could easily have gone the other way.

What next?

Don't be put off by what you have read so far! It would be unfair to make it all sound easy and rosy, especially to people who may be vulnerable, working through a separation. It is far better to start the process informed. You want to be smart and savvy, but still open to new possibilities and opportunities, while avoiding repeating problems of the past.

Try to be open about your expectations of the people you meet — you just never know what they can offer. It could be as simple as knowing a great plumber, or you may share a love of mountain biking! Enjoy the company of your date and if it's not exactly what you are looking for, you may gain something else.

However, if you are not interested in pursuing your match on any level, tell them. A simple 'thanks for meeting with me, but I don't think we have a future' is just fine — and so much better than ignoring or making up an excuse. If you receive that message yourself, don't be offended, just move on. You are not interested in someone who is not interested in you.

The reality of modern dating is that you are in the driver's seat. No guarantees, but dating offers an opportunity to rediscover yourself, at your pace, enabling you to rebuild after your break-up.

In real life — the lowdown on dating

> *After ending her relationship of over 20 years, Josie thought she was 'fine' just a few months out. A friend who had been through separation himself, years earlier, told her 'it takes three years before you will feel like yourself', and Josie realised he was right, three years later.*
>
> *At 49 she was initially happy to be alone as she was facing an uphill legal battle. Dating just seemed too hard while Josie was coming to terms with so many other aspects of her new life. After some months, however, feeling a little lonely, curiosity got the better of her.*
>
> *'With no single friends to ask, I took no advice,' says Josie. 'My first profile was long and clumsy and included nothing about what I wanted from*

dating or the gist of my personality. That didn't last long — one of the first men I met kindly pointed out my error, and I swiftly adjusted my profile and was significantly more successful!'

Josie continues: 'My initial objective was to find out if there were any men out there who would find me attractive, and then to simply practise meeting new men. That sounds easier than it was — in my relationship my husband was socially dominant, and so he introduced any new people into the relationship. My historic role was passive, and I was familiar with fading into the background, so being the focus of a date and a key member of the social interaction was difficult. But not impossible, as I quickly found.'

Forced to behave in a more socially assertive way than she had in her previous life, Josie found herself starting conversations and keeping them going, learning to say 'no' if she didn't want to continue the liaison, and accepting compliments without brushing them off.

'I'm not ashamed to say that during the course of the first few dates I quickly realised that I needed to upskill in other ways; after more than twenty years with the same man, I wanted to test myself physically — taking my clothes off with other partners being a big one to tick off — and having new experiences. I was fast reaching the end of that phase and about to move on to the next (for

me, a new relationship) when I met my new partner, but I don't regret one moment of that phase of my dating life!'

Josie learned a lot in that period. 'There were other men in that time who were keen to fit me into their futures, and I had to say no, they were not for me. I realised I was not only allowed but expected to express my own needs or desires, however awkward I found that initially.'

She continues: 'I gave my full attention to everyone I met, I came to know what their children were up to, the difficulties they were facing with aging parents, and how and why their relationships had ended. It was helpful to me to realise these were just people chatting about their lives and experiences, maybe even a little lonely — just like me — and not at all intimidating. For the first time in years, my mind was truly open. I gave everything a go and along the way gained confidence and learned my boundaries; and most importantly, I learned that I was in charge and, if I didn't want to, I didn't have to — and I said so.'

Josie had a range of experiences, both good and not so good, but along the way she 'met some amazing people who remain great friends years later.'

In real life — what does a man say?

I didn't really feel intimidated by having to start dating again after more than a decade, in fact I was quite excited by the prospect. I knew there was a risk I wouldn't find someone, but it seemed unlikely that there was no one compatible out there.

Having come out of an unrewarding relationship, matching with interesting women and going on dates helped me to feel attractive and desirable again. Even just matching with someone was a bit of a thrill. I'm sure a lot of people have come out of relationships where they no longer really engaged with their partners, so to start finding people who reciprocated and opened up with me emotionally was a great feeling.

Thinking about profiles that really interested me, I think it is better to include photos that show you doing things that you really love. In my profile, I included some information about me, but I also had a bit of a description of the attributes I was looking for. Even though I was open to a relationship, having been single for a number of years, I didn't say this specifically. I wanted to find a woman who was physically fit and looked after herself (I like to keep fit) and who was in a similar position to me in her life.

Online dating takes a lot of time and effort if you genuinely take it seriously. I spent many evenings getting to know women online. There was always someone to text or chat to, with the result that I never felt lonely or socially isolated. The women I met were, on the whole, really interesting. Other people dating are usually there following a break-up, so you have things in common such as past relationship problems and dating experiences. It's great to listen to other people's life stories.

The medium of texting makes it easier to take more emotional risk, be more edgy, and talk about things you wouldn't otherwise talk about. I guess one reason is that nothing rides on the chat — if you overstep someone's boundary and they delete you, it doesn't matter. I believe there is research which says that the people who are most successful on dating sites are the ones who took risks with their conversation.

I have, after some time, found myself in a great relationship. My new partner fits the criteria I set for myself, so long may this last!

A NEW RELATIONSHIP (WITHOUT THE OLD PROBLEMS)

NEW FRIENDSHIPS WILL FORM, old friendships may take time to settle into your new normal, and you may find yourself with a new partner. This section focuses on new partners and managing the new relationship.

Minimising your 'baggage'

'Baggage' is a word you will have heard a lot — everyone wants a simple life, and a partner with 'no baggage'. It's just not realistic to have no baggage, but it is possible to come to terms with your baggage.

If you find yourself repeating stories about your past relationship to friends, family, and dates, that's probably unresolved baggage. You may be harbouring bitterness which can follow you into your future, affecting your chance of a happy and successful relationship.

With that in mind, before forming a new relationship take the time to heal. We have talked before about how each party in a separation has some responsibility for that relationship not continuing, and by looking at yourself honestly and thoroughly in counselling, you will be able to identify what it is that you are holding on to and — more importantly — why, enabling you to avoid repetition in the future and to form new healthy relationships.

Communicating with your new partner

Did your mother tell you to 'start as you mean to go on'? Starting a new relationship with open and honest communication is a good way to avoid bad habits developing. It may be hard to begin with, but with practice is so rewarding.

It is worth spending time here to talk about how to avoid the 'destructive cycle of communication', for the sake of your new relationship. Every relationship has some natural friction which causes discomfort. This discomfort — or even pain — can be dealt with in several ways:

- confront it with a view to learning from it, or
- get angry or accusatory, or
- run.

It's pretty clear from those choices that if you can both agree to learn how to manage and grow from difficult situations, you will create an easier path forward. That doesn't mean avoiding the conflict, it means confronting it while moderating your behaviour and remaining loving and respectful to both yourself and your partner. It's not as hard as it sounds, but it requires some assertiveness training, and practice.

Assertiveness is about communicating effectively and feeling good about doing it, whether accepting a compliment, expressing your feelings, or offering constructive criticism. The best outcome from assertive behaviour is a relationship based on honesty and mutual respect. The other side of the coin is passive behaviour where you avoid conflict by ignoring your own feelings, resulting in resentment.

The key factors of assertive communication are honesty, directness, and appropriateness. Being honest with ourselves means expressing (not repressing) our needs, wants and feelings in a consistent manner so the person we are talking to doesn't have to guess. Being direct means stating our needs as clearly as possible; and appropriateness means fitting your behaviour to suit the situation, taking into account the other person's feelings.

You'd be surprised at how often assertiveness skills are needed — think about how well (or otherwise) you take a compliment; or how good you are at saying 'no'; or starting a conversation with a new person, or a difficult conversation with anyone. All require assertiveness.

If you don't respond in a positive way to a compliment, you are telling the person paying the compliment that they may as well not bother — we don't want that! Next time, just say 'thanks, that's kind'.

The feeling of losing yourself in your relationship is down to a lack of assertiveness. Not knowing how you feel is down to a lack of assertiveness. Getting walked all over and taken for granted, that's right, you guessed it. Being assertive is not appropriate in all situations, but trust me, it's worth taking the time to learn this skill before you need it again.

Children and your new partner

Introducing a new partner can make separation harder for your children because they may feel disloyal to their other parent. To help them, make time for your child to be with just you and not your new partner — it will reinforce their place with you.

Be sensitive when introducing a new partner and listen to what your children say about them. You don't have to agree, but it's important to let them have an opinion. Children need to understand you are not replacing their other parent, and that your new partner is not a parent. To reinforce that, it's best not to ask them to call the new partner Mum or Dad.

What happens if one of your children just doesn't like your new partner? Or the other way around and your new partner has no time for your child? Stress to the person having difficulties that they only need to behave in a respectful and courteous way, and there's no other obligation.

Your new partner may also have children and introducing an entire new family into your relationship with your children is challenging. You may need to be patient. Again, listen to your children when they tell you how they feel, and try to accommodate their needs.

In real life — introducing your new partner to your adult child

My Dad got a new partner just a few months into my parents' separation. I found out about her from someone else, but when I raised it with him, he was apologetic and seemed to understand how I felt. He was also respectful about introducing her to me and always made time for me to spend time with him alone, and I never felt confronted by him behaving romantically with his new partner.

Not so Mum. A year or so after the break-up, she told me about her new partner but introduced him with no warning. I have been shocked by how different her new relationship is to her relationship with Dad. While I would never want her to have another relationship like that, it was one of the constants in my life and I found the change difficult.

She was physically affectionate towards this other person which seemed somehow vulgar to me, perhaps because of its novelty. I asked her to show some restraint, but it just sounded like I didn't want her to be happy — I do. I really just wanted to be eased into this particular transition, and my needs considered.

I also wanted her to spend time with me alone, which she probably didn't really want to do because our relationship had become strained. It seemed she had found a new 'best friend' and I missed the person I knew as Mum. She had been the pivotal person in my life for ever, my friend and confidante but, having pushed through many of our issues post break-up, there was now a man in her life who she prioritised over me.

Years later, I feel lucky to have a wonderful relationship with my mother's partner and consider him an absolute bonus family member.

Why you need a new will

As you will have read in the section on financial advisers, if you have a will and *enter* a marriage or civil union, the old will is automatically revoked, unless it was clearly made in anticipation of the marriage or civil union.

However, should your marriage or civil union *end*, your will remains in force. On formal dissolution, any provisions in your will in favour of your former partner become void. Provisions appointing your former partner a trustee or executor of your will also become void. The rest of your will remains valid, in the same way it would if your former partner had died just before you.

A de facto relationship does not have the same status as a marriage or civil union when it comes to wills, and your will continues to be current until you change it. The same is true for enduring powers of attorney.

In short, along with all your other new beginnings, make a new will. You can use a simple — free — online template to avoid legal costs, or you can seek the advice of a lawyer and have them draft one for you.

Protecting yourself and your assets

Once you have been living with a new partner for three years you are officially in a de facto relationship, and the Property (Relationships) Act applies to your relationship. This effectively means that, if you separate, your new partner will have a claim on your assets, and vice versa.

(As an aside, keep a note of key dates. From a legal standpoint, it is useful to record the date you started living with your new partner and the date you stopped living together.)

If your assets were held in a family trust prior to living together with your new partner, those assets will have the protection of the trust should things not work out. If you don't have the protection of a trust, any lawyer or financial adviser will tell you that a Contracting Out Agreement is a must. There's more detail in the legal section about this, but essentially these agreements allow you to set your own rules for ownership and division of property in the event the relationship breaks down. A Contracting Out Agreement recognises financial contributions when purchasing an asset and records the assets each party brings into the relationship, effectively acting as an insurance policy against separation.

Like your will, a Contracting Out Agreement is a 'living document'. It should be reviewed every five years or so to ensure it is still fair. If, because of changes in the relationship, it becomes unfair, it is unlikely to hold up in court should the relationship break down.

Hopefully, in the first year or two of your new relationship you will have established good communication mechanisms and will be able to have one of those open and honest conversations about this relatively easily. Remember, it's important for both parties.

It's great that you have fallen in love, just be savvy about it!

CHECKLIST FOR SEPARATION

- Check in with yourself — are you sure this is what you want? Maybe seek counselling or even see a lawyer to discuss.
- Ask for support from trusted friends and family.
- Always first, what do the children need to get through this? Form a plan about where they will live and who they will live with initially.
- Are you staying on in the home you shared with your former partner? If so, create some privacy for yourself and ask for their agreement not to enter without being invited in.
- Look at your finances and sort out where the funds to pay the bills will be coming from — for both parties to the separation. There may be financial support you are entitled to, particularly where children are involved.
- Gather or download all your important

documents — tax returns, bank statements, ownership documentation, personal documents such as passport(s).
- Find out your legal position and the steps you need to take. Even if you can agree to separate amicably, it pays to at least know the law.
- Make a list of assets, divided into separate and relationship property, and agree it with your former partner. There will be items each of you want to keep ownership of, and there may be some items you both want to keep. In the scheme of this tumultuous change in your life, pick your battles.
- Open a bank account in your sole name and get agreement that neither one of you will access joint funds without the consent of the other.
- Move any direct debits you are paying for personally to your bank account and contact utility providers to change the name on accounts to your name only. Similarly with medical and dental contacts.
- If you don't have your own email address, set one up, and while you are doing it change any passwords to ensure your privacy.
- Change your will and enduring powers of attorney.
- Post financial separation, break joint accounts and transfer bank and credit card suppliers, utilities, and phone/broadband providers to your own name. The same goes for any assets or

investments, including any vehicle you are keeping. For shares and property, you will need the cooperation of your former partner to sign documents to effect the transfer.

THE LAST WORD

I HOPE you have found what you were seeking in this book — practical advice enabling you to get through and start afresh, confident and informed.

It has been an interesting process, researching and writing. I have continued to learn, benefiting my relationships with my children and new partner. Unexpectedly, I have also come to understand my former partner's reactions and emotions and to make peace with my past.

To buy further copies for friends starting on this path (or your former partner), please visit www.uncoupling.guide and order online. All the best with your journey.

ACKNOWLEDGMENTS

As we each worked through our financial separation, my old friend Lynne Fleury thought others would benefit from the lessons we had learned. I'm so grateful to her for supporting this endeavour to put her idea into practice.

Thank you to the women and men, friends and strangers, who have shared their deeply personal stories. Their time and energy reliving and sharing past relationship hurt hopefully helped to heal that hurt.

My thanks also to the many experts who have filled the gaps in my knowledge. And my small, wise book club. Every author needs a book club.

My adult children have supported me through every foolish and not so foolish endeavour since I separated from their father. They have been forced to grow up a bit more quickly than would have been ideal but have come out of it more resilient and self-sufficient than I could have hoped.

The list (and the book) wouldn't be complete without my new partner, a constant source of encouragement and positivity, not to mention a moderating influence on my wilder ideas! His own relationship issues and his personal experiences gave me perspective which I hope is apparent in this book.

ABOUT THE AUTHOR

Barbara Relph became a professional writer and editor in 2017 when her separation forced her to re-think her life. Now a true digital nomad, she travels between rural Manawatu and central Auckland, armed with her laptop, living her best life.

When Barbara realised there were no practical guides written on separation, she gathered together the excellent advice and stories, both professional and personal, from those who helped her navigate the complicated process of uncoupling. And wrote it down for you.

www.uncoupling.guide

 facebook.com/UncouplingNZ